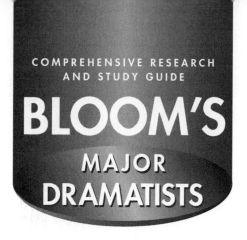

COMPREHENSIVE RESEARCH
AND STUDY GUIDE

BLOOM'S

MAJOR
DRAMATISTS

Sam Shepard

EDITED AND WITH AN
INTRODUCTION BY HAROLD BLOOM

CURRENTLY AVAILABLE

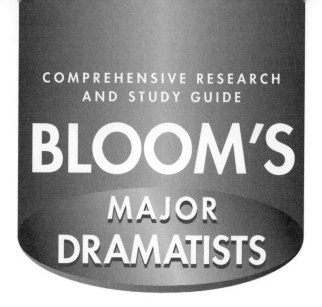

COMPREHENSIVE RESEARCH
AND STUDY GUIDE

BLOOM'S
MAJOR
DRAMATISTS

Sam
Shepard

EDITED AND WITH AN INTRODUCTION
BY HAROLD BLOOM

CHELSEA HOUSE
PUBLISHERS
A Haights Cross Communications Company

Philadelphia

Printed and bound in the United States of America.

First Printing
1 3 5 7 9 8 6 4 2

Library of Congress Cataloging-in-Publication Data
Sam Shepard / editor, Harold Bloom ; contributing editor, Anne Marie
Albertazzi
        p. cm. —(Bloom's major dramatists)
Includes bibliographical references and index.
    ISBN 0-7910-7035-2
    1.Shepard, Sam, 1943– —Criticism and interpretation.   I. Bloom,
Harold. II. Albertazzi, Anne Marie. III. Series
    PS3569.H394 Z86 2002
    812'.54—dc21   2002008450

Chelsea House Publishers
1974 Sproul Road, Suite 400
Broomall, PA 19008-0914

http://www.chelseahouse.com

Contributing Editor: Anne Marie Albertazzi

Cover designed by Terry Mallon

Layout by EJB Publishing Services

CONTENTS

USER'S GUIDE

This volume is designed to present biographical, critical, and bibliographical information on the author and the author's best-known or most important plays. Following Harold Bloom's editor's note and introduction is a concise biography of the author that discusses major life events and important literary accomplishments. A critical analysis of each play follows, tracing significant themes, patterns, and motifs in the work. An annotated list of characters supplies brief information on the main characters in each play.

A selection of critical extracts, derived from previously published material, follows each thematic analysis. In most cases, these extracts represent the best analysis available from a number of leading critics. Because these extracts are derived from previously published material, they will include the original notations and references when available. Each extract is cited, and readers are encouraged to use the original publications as they continue their research. A bibliography of the author's writings, a list of additional books and articles on the author and their work, and an index of themes and ideas conclude the volume.

As with any study guide, this volume is designed as a supplement to the works being discussed, and is in no way intended as a replacement for those works. The reader is advised to read the text prior to using this study guide, and to keep it accessible for quick reference.

ABOUT THE EDITOR

Harold Bloom is Sterling Professor of the Humanities at Yale University and Henry W. and Albert A. Berg Professor of English at the New York University Graduate School. He is the author of over 20 books, and the editor of more than 30 anthologies of literary criticism.

Professor Bloom's works include *Shelley's Mythmaking* (1959), *The Visionary Company* (1961), *Blake's Apocalypse* (1963), *Yeats* (1970), *A Map of Misreading* (1975), *Kabbalah and Criticism* (1975), *Agon: Toward a Theory of Revisionism* (1982), *The American Religion* (1992), *The Western Canon* (1994), and *Omens of Millennium: The Gnosis of Angels, Dreams, and Resurrection* (1996). *The Anxiety of Influence* (1973) sets forth Professor Bloom's provocative theory of the literary relationships between the great writers and their predecessors. His most recent books include *Shakespeare: The Invention of the Human*, a 1998 National Book Award finalist, *How to Read and Why* (2000), and *Stories and Poems for Extremely Intelligent Children of All Ages* (2001).

Professor Bloom earned his Ph.D. from Yale University in 1955 and has served on the Yale faculty since then. He is a 1985 MacArthur Foundation Award recipient and served as the Charles Eliot Norton Professor of Poetry at Harvard University in 1987–88. In 1999 he was awarded the prestigious American Academy of Arts and Letters Gold Medal for Criticism. Professor Bloom is the editor of several other Chelsea House series in literary criticism, including BLOOM'S MAJOR SHORT STORY WRITERS, BLOOM'S MAJOR NOVELISTS, BLOOM'S MAJOR DRAMATISTS, BLOOM'S MODERN CRITICAL INTERPRETATIONS, BLOOM'S MODERN CRITICAL VIEWS, and BLOOM'S BIOCRITIQUES.

EDITOR'S NOTE

My Introduction considers Shepard as an American Original and touches upon *Fool For Love*, my favorite among his plays.

Ellen Oumano illuminates the circumstances surrounding the writing of *Zabriskie Point*, after which Mel Gussow discusses concepts of family and identity in *Burried Child*.

Tucker Orbison, among others, considers *True West*'s Austin and Lee to be dual representations on the self, while Jeffrey D. Hoeper discusses the similarities between the two brothers and their biblical predecessors, Cain and Able. This volume's final play, *Fool for Love*, is seen by Frank Rich as a skillful reinvention of the lost American West.

Harold Bloom

Incest, according to Shelley, is the most poetical of circumstances. This brief prelude to Sam Shepard centers upon *Fool for Love*, which I like best of his several dozen plays. Walt Whitman, an authentic forerunner of Shepard, denied being influenced by anyone, though without Ralph Waldo Emerson one can doubt Whitman would have happened. Shepard similarly denies all literary and dramatic indebtedness, insisting he emanates from Jackson Pollack and the Who. Plays however are written with words, and Shepard, if your perspective is long enough, is another Expressionist dramatist, a very good one, with a definite relation to "Brecht"! The quotation marks are there because we know that most of "Brecht" was written by two very talented women whom the rascal exploited.

Shepard also shows some touches of Pinter, and even of Pinter's precursor, Beckett. There seems no clear American lineage in dramatic tradition for the very American Shepard. I find a touch of Tennessee Williams in Martin, May's date in *Fool for Love*, and dimly in the background are the Strindbergian asperities of Eugene O'Neill's destructive family romances. Yet no one can dispute that Sam Shepard is an American Original. Emerson, everyone's American grandfather, told us: "The originals are not original." Rock and roll performers, whom Shepard so envies, all have their formative phases, in which their ancestry is quite clear, the Who included. Shepard, who battles so fiercely against categorization, resembles a tradition in American literature that R.W.B. Lewis has called Adamic. Like Walt Whitman, Sam Shepard seeks to be Adam early in the morning, but a Western American Adam.

Fool for Love has four characters, all American archetypes. The incestuous lovers, May and Eddie, are half-siblings; Eddie is a dead-end cowboy. May, a drifter, is caught up with Eddie in a hopelessly ambivalent relationship, always about to end but unable to do so. Their common father, the Old Man, is dead, but highly visible, at least to us in the audience. He too is a cowboy, rocking away and consuming whiskey beyond the grave. That leaves only Martin, May's would-be date, who appears to be a surrogate for the audience.

Everything about *Fool for Love* suggests a controlled hallucination. Nothing is certain, least of all incest; since the Old Man insists he sees nothing of himself in either of the lovers. Nor can we believe anything that May and Eddie say about one another. We can be certain that they inspire obsessiveness, each in himself or herself and in the (more-or-less) beloved.

The paradox in Shepard is why any of his people matter, to us or to him. The answer, which confers aesthetic dignity, is altogether Whitmanian. *Song of Myself* anticipates Shepard: his burned-out Americans were Whitman's before they were Shepard's. Walt Whitman, the true American shaman, would have been at home in *Fool for Love*, *Buried Child*, and *True West*.

Shepard's people are lyrical selves, desperately seeking a stable identity. They are not going to find it. Their dramatist remains our major living visionary, stationed at the edge of our common abyss.

Sam Shepard

Sam Shepard is one of America's most prolific dramatists, as well as a screenplay writer, memoirist, and successful film actor. A former cowboy, a recluse, and a skeptic of corporate sponsored theatre, his work nevertheless has placed him in the spotlight and his personal charisma has made him a film star. Since his off-off Broadway days on the Lower East Side of New York City, his irreverent, satirical and nostalgic treatment of American popular culture has attracted a cult following as well as the respect of critics and theatergoers alike.

Shepard's work draws from American traditions such as rock and country music, western movies, science fiction, and horror stories. His satirical and experimental style is due in large part to the 1960's counterculture that influenced him during his early years in New York. A familiar theme in Shepard's work is the demise of the American frontier myth, with its archetypal masculinity, as represented by the now anachronistic cowboy. In addition, he is recognized for his ability to create characters that seem mired in a place between a romanticized past and a bleak present that is replete with incest, alcoholism, and a surreal loss of identity and origin.

Sam Shepard was born Samuel Shepard Rogers III in Fort Sheridan, Illinois on November 5, 1943. Nicknamed "Steve," he grew up on his family's avocado ranch in Duarte, California, where the agrarian life molded both his own persona and that of the characters he would create in his plays. Holding jobs such as stable hand, sheep shearer, and orange picker, and winning the grand prize at the Los Angeles County fair for his yearling ram, Shepard treaded a path toward veterinary medicine and attended Mount San Antonio Junior College in 1961 as an agricultural science major. However, when his alcoholic father's drinking worsened and his family life became too complicated, Shepard left home to join a theatrical group called the Bishop's Company Repertory Players. In 1963 he moved to New York City, where he changed his name from Steve Rogers to Sam Shepard.

In New York, Shepard supported himself as a busboy, waiter, and musician while writing plays. He joined the off-off-Broadway movement of New York's Lower East Side, and was influenced specifically by the avant-garde techniques of the experimental Open Theater, whose resistance to conventional dramatic resolution included the technique of "transformations," in which characters changed personalities between scenes. In 1964 Shepard's one-act plays *Cowboys* and *The Rock Garden* were produced at Theatre Genesis on the Lower East Side. During the following season, in 1965, his next three plays *Chicago*, *Icarus' Mother*, and *Red Cross* earned the Village Voice's Obie Awards for best plays off-Broadway. Continuing to develop his talent for representing life in a disturbingly surreal manner, he wrote numerous plays for experimental theaters such as Caffé Cino, La Mama, and the American Palace Theater. Of these, his first full-length play *La Turista* (1967), based on the pun on the Mexican word for tourist and the name of the illness many travelers get in Mexico, won an Obie Award. Shepard was now known for his ability to shock the avant-garde scene with his use of disorientation and fantasy and his flair for representing the frontier myth and other elements of popular culture in unsettling and satirical ways. In *The Unseen Hand* (1969), each character suffers the threat of unseen hands, and *Mad Dog Blues* (1971) is a treasure hunt adventure-comedy that mingles legendary characters such as Mae West, Jesse James and Marlene Dietrich.

Living in London between 1971 and 1974, Shepard wrote several plays that were successful in both London and New York, especially *The Tooth of Crime* (1972), a rock drama, and *Geography of a Horse Dreamer* (1974), whose idea came from watching English dog racing. Both plays explored the predicament of the artist when faced with the seductive pull of commercialism. Back in the United States, he wrote *Curse of the Starving Class* (1976), about the darkly humorous spectacle of American family life, which departed from his earlier surrealistic style and began a new phase of realism.

Gaining even more critical attention, Shepard received the Pulitzer Prize for *Buried Child* (1978) and accolades for *True West* (1980); these two plays joined *Curse of the Starving Class* to make up what Shepard called his "family trilogy," so named because they share common themes about familial strife. His many theatrical works in the 1980's and 1990's include *Fool for Love* (1983), *A Lie of the Mind* (1985), which won the New York Drama Critics Circle Award, *States of Shock* (1991), and *Simpatico* (1994). Most recently, *The Late Henry Moss*, a play about two brothers who meet in the desert over the death of their father and confront their violent past, premiered in San Francisco in 2000 and New York in 2001.

In addition to his theatrical works, Shepard has written over fifteen screenplays, including *Paris, Texas* (1984), which was adapted from his book of reminiscences *Motel Chronicles* (1982) and received the Golden Palm Award at Cannes Film Festival. Other screenplays include *Far North* (1988) and *Silent Tongue* (1993), both of which he also directed. He was inducted into the Theatre Hall of Fame in 1994. Shepard has acted in over thirty films, including *Raggedy Man* (1981), *Frances* (1982), and *The Right Stuff* (1983), for which he received an Oscar nomination. Most recently, he has starred in *Snow Falling on Cedars* (1999) and *Black Hawk Down* (2001). He will star in the upcoming *Leopold Bloom* (to be released in 2003), and his new collection of short stories, *Great Dream of Heaven*, is set to be published in 2002.

Sam Shepard married O-Lan Johnson, an actress in Theater Genesis, in 1969. They had a son named Jesse Mojo and were later divorced. Shepard also has two children, Hannah Jane and Samuel Walker, with actress Jessica Lange.

PLOT SUMMARY OF

Zabriskie Point

Zabriskie Point, expensive to make and assailed by most critics, was
considered a cinematic disaster at the time of its release in 1970.
Much was expected of its director, Michelangelo Antonioni, whose
1966 film *Blow-Up* had been a major success, but the film was
judged as falling short of his potential. Nevertheless, *Zabriskie Point*
remains a cult favorite and serves as an important artifact of the
Vietnam era and of avant-garde filmmaking. Sam Shepard co-wrote
the screenplay with Michelangelo Antonioni, Tonino Guerra, Fred
Gardner, who was a liberal journalist and activist, and Clare Peploe,
who was Antonioni's companion at the time.

The film plays out the conflict between the rebellious, idealistic,
vulnerable youth and their staid, conservative, oppressive elders;
between revolutionary chaos and authoritarian control; and between
the raw power of the western frontier and the profiteering might of
the culture that appropriates it. Also at stake is the internal conflict
within youths who came of age during the 1960's, as exemplified by
the central character, Mark. He tries to define a life, paradoxically,
by the ideals he will die for, and he is faced with the decision
between doing battle with the establishment and escaping it all
through drugs or some other flight. The disorientation that Mark
experiences is a combination of distrust for the older generation,
alienation from his own, and a hallucinatory experience with nature.
It is questionable whether his death is a heroic statement or a random
casualty. As such, *Zabriskie Point* is a reflection of the time in which
it is made. Yet it also contains elements that have a wider resonance
and carry into Shepard's other works: the conflict between the
younger and older generations, the satirical treatment of corporate
greed and commercial imperialism, and the portrayal of the
American frontier as a powerful ghost.

As the film begins, a group of black and white college students
are planning a protest at their school. They debate over what it
means to be a revolutionary, and racial differences fuel the dispute.
Feeling tyrannized by the police presence at the school, they plan to
close the school down and keep it closed until authorities answer to

their terms. Two black students lead the campaign to use guerilla tactics and stop at nothing, including the use of deadly weapons and homemade bombs, to achieve their end. However, despite all of the debate, it is never revealed what the students are fighting for, which adds an element of absurdity to the scene.

One student asks the question: "Are you willing to die?" A white male student, Mark, stands up and says he would die, but when further questioned he eschews the meeting as boring and walks out, leaving his roommate to defend him to the indignant group. A critical student argues that in order to be a revolutionary, one has to learn how to work with other people, citing Lenin, Castro, and even anarchists. Another student says that Mark was practicing "bourgeois individualism," which will get him killed. This comment casts a prophetic shadow on Mark, who represents the element of this generation that is ultimately doomed.

In the next scene, Daria, another college-aged youth, runs into the lobby of the Sunny Dunes Land Development Company and asks a security guard if she can be admitted to retrieve a book she left there while filling in for a secretary. When she asks the skeptical security guard who can give her permission, he points to Lee Allen, a company executive, who hears her story. Allen offers her a job at Sunny Dunes, which she accepts.

As Mark drives his roommate to school, he claims that students talk about violence rather than use it. He, on the other hand, will act on his beliefs. He goes to the jail to bail his friend out and ends up being booked for disobeying orders to leave. As the policeman books him, Mark gives the name Carl Marx. The other students laugh as the unsuspecting policeman asks him how to spell it. As is evident in this scene and others, the film is sympathetic to the youth culture, who are portrayed as free and adventurous in spirit, despite their imprisonment by an unthinking, authoritarian establishment. Later, Mark and his friend use the establishment's bigotry against them: they buy two '38's at a gun store, and get past the 4-5 day check by insinuating to the racist clerk that they will be defending their women from non-whites.

In a satirical segment that follows, executives of a Sunny Dunes Land Development Company view their commercial, which features stiff mannequins posed in different costumes on their beautiful desert properties. Later, Allen and his colleague listen to the radio in the car and hear of Vietnam casualties, mass uprooting of residents due to freeway development, and a militant student protest at California State College that resulted in 27 arrests. However, the only news that interests the two executives is that New York still has more millionaires than California.

Simultaneously hearing this newscast on the radio in an apartment, Mark leaves for the college campus, hiding his new gun in his boot. Back at Sunny Dunes Development Company, Allen finds that his secretary, Daria, is gone. We see her driving with a map on a desert highway. Allen calls Daria's number and finds out from a strange boy that she has disappeared with his car.

On the college campus, policemen are fighting off protesters, and students bloodied by the combat are carried off. Police surround a building that is being occupied by protesters. Mark arrives and hides behind a building where the policemen's backs are in view. When the police throw tear gas into the building, four black students emerge and surrender, but another is shot by the police for supposedly having a gun. Mark aims his gun at one of the policemen, and a shot rings out as the policeman falls dead. Mark then runs away, rides a bus to the end of the line, and calls his roommate from a pay phone, who tells him that people on TV are saying that the policeman's killer looks just like Mark. Mark hangs up and follows a plane's trajectory to an aviation club, where he steals a small plane and flies it away toward the desert. When he sees Daria's car moving along the desert highway, he begins flying low over her car, circling back, and doing the same thing again. Later he lands the plane and they meet. He asks her for a ride. They drive to Zabriskie Point, a spot in Death Valley described on a sign as "an area of Ancient lake beds deposited five to ten million years ago. These beds have been tilted and pushed upward by earth forces, and eroded by wind and water." Presented here is a metaphor of social change, an ancient process in which the old gives way to the new. As the new generation ferments, agitates, and pushes upward, it causes the old to erode away, only to follow it in turn.

As the two talk, Mark tells Daria that he had been kicked out of school for breaking into the dean's office and reprogramming his computer to make all the engineers take art courses. He asks her about the protests and she says that she heard on the radio that a cop was killed by a white man. They climb down into the lakebed and play, and then make love. As they do, several couples seem to come out of the dust and make love in pairs and threesomes around them. Afterwards, they vanish. The ghostly lovers in this scene were portrayed by members of the Open Theater, an avant-garde repertory group with whom Shepard was closely connected in the late 1960's and early 1970's.

Mark and Daria walk to a pair of outhouses; when a policeman approaches, Mark points his gun at him from behind an outhouse, though the policeman never sees it and drives away. This prompts Daria to ask Mark if he shot the cop in the protest. Mark sullenly admits that he lost his chance to make the hit because someone did it before him.

Mark commissions Daria and an old man to help him repaint the plane so he can drive it back to L.A. and return it before being found out. He flies away and Daria heads to Phoenix, her original destination. As Mark lands in L.A., police shoot at his plane for evading them and kill him. Daria hears of his death on her car radio. She continues on to Allen's house in Phoenix, shaken. Instead of staying with Allen—who at this point may be her lover—she heads to her car. As she looks at the house, she imagines it exploding over and over. Lawn furniture, clothes, refrigerators, books, and other symbols of consumer culture explode into the air repeatedly. At this point she has switched her loyalty from the capitalistic tycoon to Mark and the student protesters. She smiles and leaves.

Zabriskie Point

Mark is a loner and social rebel who is dedicated to change but distrusts organized movements. His dissatisfaction with student movements and his unwillingness to run from the law both come from a professed belief that one must take risks and not expect to fail. After failing to shoot a policeman who killed a protester at his school, he steals a small plane and heads out on his own, under the pretext that he was expelled for illegally reprogramming the dean's computer. Yet his motives are ultimately childish; when matters become serious or deadly, as when he has the chance to kill a cop or when Daria suggests a death game at Zabriskie Point, he loses his drive. He is suspended in a mentality of play, and succeeds only in teasing authority—messing with computers, using Carl Marx's name when he is arrested, and driving by police cars with his middle finger in the air. Mark is killed by policemen when he lands the stolen plane in L.A., more likely a testament to his naivete about the strength of his enemy than a mark of heroism.

Daria is a college-aged girl who is not at all involved in political affairs and would rather listen to music than the news. She gets a job working for Lee Allen at Sunny Dunes Land Development Company when he spots her in the lobby of his building, after which she disappears into the California desert with a friend's car. When she meets Mark in the desert, her lackadaisical attitude toward social activism and her preference for smoking marijuana and meditation provide a contrast to his rebelliousness. Her job at Sunny Dunes, embellished perhaps by a love affair with Lee Allen, aligns her with the older generation. Yet after Daria learns that Mark dies, she effects an escape of her own, leaving Allen's home in the desert and imagining that it explodes repeatedly. In this sense she has placed her loyalty with Mark and the generation of students who denounce capitalism.

Lee Allen is an executive at Sunny Dunes Land Development Company, the evil center of capitalism, commercialism and disrespect for nature. His skyscraper office, slick plastic commercials, and sumptuous desert home represent the social ills that the protesting students are trying to eliminate. He and his colleague care more about the number of millionaires in New York than they do about the massive destruction brought on by the Vietnam war and the student protests against it; thus, he represents the materialistic poison that the students believe contaminates their world.

Kathleen is a black student activist who leads the meeting shown at the beginning of the story. She believes that black students are true revolutionaries because they have suffered more oppression, and that the only way to effect change is through the use of "guerilla tactics." She proposes a strategy of secret, surprise attacks in which "the enemy is invisible," so that when injury or destruction occurs, there will be no one to blame.

CRITICAL VIEWS ON

Zabriskie Point

VINCENT CANBY ON THE FILM'S TWO FANTASY SCENES

[Vincent Canby (1924-2000) was the *New York Times'* senior film critic from 1969 to 1993 and the author of *Living Quarters* (1975) and *Unnatural Scenery* (1979). In this excerpt, Canby recounts the sex scene and the final explosion scene with both delight and derision.]

Antonioni has never been one to let his actors do much in the way of acting (he calls that "rhetoric") but he has, on occasion, made magnificent use of an individual performer's emotional equipment as reflected in the way he or she simply looks or moves. For "Zabriskie Point," he chose two young people who have never acted before and who, though they are quite beautiful, register on film as complete cyphers. This may be because of their lack of experience, or because in real life they don't move particularly well or naturally. Whatever the reason, there is hardly a gesture, or a way of reading speech, that doesn't seem to have been imposed on them from without.

In all of Antonioni's films, there are evidences of the struggle going on between Antonioni-the-spontaneous-filmmaker and Antonioni-the-intellectual-filmmaker. In his greatest film, "L'Avventura," the two opposing forces achieve a perfect balance. The psychological substructure matches the intellectual superstructure. "Zabriskie Point" is nothing but superstructure, as a result of which his characters begin to look very much like the life-size mannequins who perform in a grotesque television commercial within the film.

I'm not especially offended by what Antonioni has to say about the state of this country, and I really don't think his primary interest is condemning an affluent, materialistic society that offers no positive choices to its young people. Rather, he is trying to say this is the way it looks and the way it *feels* to be here now. However, I am offended by the quite ordinary images he uses— of Death Valley, and of poor, old, maligned Los Angeles with its used-car lots, its absurd billboards and its glass-and-steel mono- liths poking their heads above the smog so beloved by Bob Hope. Even more offensive are two peculiar fantasies he sticks into the movie as projections of his own state of mind.

The first occurs when Mark and Daria make love on a sand dune and Death Valley suddenly erupts with life and love. Bodies (members of Joe Chaikin's Open Theater), mostly in discreet undress (although there are a couple of quick glimpses of geni- talia), writhe in various combinations of couplings while the screen goes deep tan, as if everything were being seen in a sand- storm. After the climax, when Antonioni has returned the sky over Death Valley to its natural, crystalline state, Mark says with the sort of satisfaction with which he might have enjoyed his first orange Julius: "I somehow always knew it would be like that."

The second fantasy—Daria's hallucination of the destruction of the Western world (in the form of Taylor's desert home, a Frank Lloyd Wright structure as it might be imitated by a housing project architect)—is a triumph by the special effects man. Nothing that has been shown in the film supports such an hallucination, but it's nice to see what can be done by a director with a big budget.

The house explodes no less than a dozen times, in increasing close-up, followed by odd, slow-motion studies of books disintegrating, the poolside terrace, the clothes closets, a television set, and even the larder. I especially liked the latter, in which the screen suddenly becomes filled with food, including a box of Kellog's K, a can of Campbell's soup, a loaf of Wonder bread, bits and pieces of lettuce, and, down-screen right, one scrawny chicken. They hang suspended, as if in some marvelous, blue emulsion. Definitely passed is the era in filmmaking, especially in avant-garde filmmaking, when a director could make do by using that tired old stock-shot of the Bikini atoll H-bomb blast.

—Vincent Canby, "No Life in Antonioni's Death Valley." *The New York Times*, 13 February 1970. *The New York Times Film Reviews* (1969-1970): 133-134.

[Richard Goldstein is a writer for the *The New York Times*. In this excerpt, Goldstein argues that the film panders to the "Woodstock Generation" and is a commercialistic scheme in itself.]

Preview night at a new Antonioni film feels a little like playing bingo in Saint Peter's Basilica. You can sense the stakes in the air, the rustle of reputation over pile carpeting, the perspiration under corporate collars. After all, this isn't just somebody's movie they're unveiling tonight. "Zabriskie Point" is MGM's entree into The New York Review of Books, and Antonioni's bid for a lifetime subscription to Rat. No wonder the lobby of the Coronet is brimming with dry expectation. One man's tenure as arbiter of Now is on the line. (...)

But the social ritual is muted tonight. What really matters at this screening is not the audience, or even the film we are about to see, but those twin spirits lurking in the projection booth. I mean the spirits of corporate desperation and youthful opposition, which seem destined to meet on screen this year in a graceful pas de deux. There are at least a dozen "youth films" on the boards in Hollywood, each designed to embrace what producers like to call the Woodstock Generation (perhaps because it's easiest for a promoter to understand new culture in terms of its most publicized event).

In terms of their commercial intent, however, it is clear that these films are meant not only to supply the youth market but—in the finest tradition of consumer culture—to create demand. To create an allegiance between youth and films which is as lucrative as the bond between youth and the record industry. If it takes raunch and revolution to bring the longhairs in, we will have it, and if it takes the Personal Cinema, we will have that too.

Which brings us to MGM, that old luxury liner of the silver screen, now encrusted with barnacles and fading Beverly Hills splendor. It's not hard to imagine what the boys in the front office wanted from Antonioni. A film which would propel the studio into a dynamic new image, killing forever the memory of "Gigi" in the minds of the young. A film which would out-cool "Easy Rider," outrage "Medium Cool," and out-swagger "Putney Swope." A film which would skirt both X and G ratings and come out R for Relevant. A film which would Americanize the mystique of Antonioni's "Blow-Up", bring all that cheeky anguish stateside and beef it up with enough rock music to insure a hot album for the studio's record division (also in dire need of overhaul).

It wouldn't be the first time an ailing institution turned to commissioned art as a bridge to the New Age. But there was something sinister about the union between Metro and Michelangelo—something about the thought of Jim Aubrey getting the bills for Antonioni's painting Death Valley white, which sent shudders down the spines of most cinéastes.

No wonder a snicker spread across this audience as the first image in Michelangelo Antonioni's first American film came into view. It was the realization that even in the New Hollywood, where the auteur rules, what comes first is that same old lion delivering the same paunchy roar.

—Richard Goldstein, "Did Antonioni Miss the 'Point'?" *The New York Times*, 22 February 1970. *The New York Times Film Reviews* (1969-1970): 137.

ELLEN OUMANO ON SHEPARD'S RELATIONSHIP WITH FILM DIRECTOR ANTONIONI

[Ellen Oumano is author of *Film Forum: Thirty-Five Top Filmmakers Discuss Their Craft* (1985), *Movies for a Desert Isle: Forty-Two Well-Known Film Lovers in Search of Their Favorite Movie (1987)*, and *Paul Newman* (1989). In this excerpt from her biography of Sam Shepard, Oumano tells the story of Shepard's involvement with the film's director, Michelangelo Antonioni.]

Nineteen sixty-eight was a wildly exciting year for Shepard, fertile and full of opportunities and challenges. Unfortunately, it also contained the seeds of great frustration. Michelangelo Antonioni, the great Italian filmmaker, asked Shepard to script his first film set and shot in America, *Zabriskie Point*. Since its subject was young American revolutionaries and it involved an airplane, it was apparently fitting that Antonioni would call upon America's premier Angry Young Man playwright, who, as it happened, had even written a play involving an airplane (*Icarus's Mother*). "He got in touch with me," Shepard told the *Village Voice*. "He came to New York looking for writers for this scenario and he read my plays. I had a play called *Icarus's Mother*, which had an airplane in it; he figured that since he had an airplane in his movie we had something in common." Shepard went to Rome to work on the script with Antonioni, and, for the first time, luxuriated in comparatively big money and a liberal expense account, courtesy of the producing studio, MGM. Both Shepard and Antonioni were blissfully ignorant of the fact that ideologically they were poles apart. Antonioni, following the fashion of the chic European left, was rhapsodic about the emerging American radical left, while Shepard held both the establishment and the rabble-rousing revolutionaries equally in contempt.

At the same time that Shepard and Antonioni and assorted others were busily working out a script, Cole was negotiating with Ted Mann for a Broadway production, possibly at the Henry Miller Theater, of one of Shepard's plays. Though he was excited at the prospect, Shepard never wavered from his primary concern that his work be served: He was adamantly opposed to a double bill with ordinary Broadway pap, insistent that Jacques Levy, whom he trusted, direct, and that no changes be made other than those authorized by either Levy or himself. The negotiations did not work out, further nurturing Shepard's growing disenchantment with "professional" theater.

Offers were pouring in—including a request to script *Alice's Restaurant*, the quintessential Sixties hippie movie starring Arlo Guthrie—but Shepard's commitment to Antonioni overrode them all.

While Shepard was in Rome, however, he met a man who asked him to help script a movie for the Rolling Stones. Thrilled, Shepard went off to Keith Richards's English estate to work on the film, to be called *Maxagasm*.

Opportunity seemed to be not merely politely knocking at his door but banging and screaming to be let in. Shepard welcomed adventure, but when he opened the door, he stepped through into thin air—a sheer drop. Everything fell through. Shepard never made it to Broadway—in fact, he never has, and deliberately so. The Rolling Stones film was never produced, and the Antonioni period was, at best, a lesson hard learned. "Antonioni contacted Shepard because he wanted a writer who understood American idiom, but he didn't understand that what Shepard wrote was Shepard's," says Bill Hart. "I think almost all of it was not used, but Shepard never made a big deal about it, he never fussed." The writing credits ended up listing Shepard, Antonioni, Fred Gardner, Clare Peploe, and Tonino Guerra. Shepard made an unsuccessful attempt to protest the credits, but it was no great loss: As one reviewer put it, the film was bad enough "to give anti-Americanism a bad name."

In the *Village Voice* interview Shepard himself spoke of the Antonioni experience as a disaster: "I wrote the version of *Zabriskie Point*, and as Antonioni got into it, he got more and more politically oriented. I didn't want anything to do with it, so I dropped out of that. However, he used quite a bit of my original stuff, up to the point where it begins to speak for radical politics.

"Antonioni wanted to make a political statement about contemporary youth, write in a lot of Marxist jargon and Black Panther speeches. I couldn't do it. I just wasn't interested.

"Plus I was twenty-four and just wasted by the experience. It was like a nightmare, I was surrounded by MGM and all that stuff.

"I like Michelangelo a lot—he is incredible—but to submerge yourself in that world of limousines and hotels and rehashing and pleasing Carlo Ponti is just ... forget it. I spent two years, off and on, around the whole business."

Though Shepard's work on *Zabriskie Point* was over when they began the shoot in Los Angeles, he spent time on the set. Michael Smith, the *Village Voice* critic whose rave review had sparked Shepard's early success, remembers visiting Shepard on the set: "It was funny—they had a whole sleek office set built up on a roof of a building in downtown Los Angeles, and they were waiting for the weather to be clear enough so they could get a shot of some building in the background. A typical movie day where they stand around and wait.

"Sam was playing with the Holy Modal Rounders at the time and sharing a house with them somewhere in Los Angeles. He was more involved with that and was just hanging around the movie set that day, checking in out of curiosity rather than working on it."

—Ellen Oumano, *Sam Shepard: the Life and Work of an American Dreamer*, (New York: St. Martin's Press, 1986): 69-72.

FIONA A. VILLELLA ON THE FILM'S AVANT-GARDE ELEMENTS

[Fiona A. Villella is a Melbourne-based writer on film. In this excerpt, Villella argues that the film challenges our sense of reality in a surrealistic and experimental fashion.]

The films pose a subject (only to compromise it), constitute objects (only to dissolve them), propose stories (only to lose them), but, equally, they turn those compromises and losses back towards another solidity... a wandering away from narrative to the surface into which it was dissolved, but in such a way that the surface takes on a fascination, becomes a "subject" all its own.
Sam Rhodie[1]

Sam Rhodie was absolutely right when he claimed that Antonioni, like no other filmmaker, introduced into the narrative fiction film elements and impulses that were purely experimental.[2] The story-lines in his films gradually dissolve and fizzle away as his real concerns take shape, and there transpires an abstraction of objects and reality, a shift to another level of seeing and, by extension, thinking.

A true art cinema director, Antonioni's distinct thematic concerns and visual concepts persist throughout his oeuvre: from the trilogy (*L'avventura* [1960], *La Notte* [1961], *L'eclisse* [1962]) to *Il Deserto Rosso* (1964) to *Zabriskie Point* to *Beyond the Clouds* (1995). Early in his filmmaking career, he was accused by critics and audiences alike of making films that were without social meaning, impact or purpose, that were nothing more than futile exercises in empty formalism. He stood out from the neo-realist practice of filmmaking that dominated Italian cinema at the time.

For Antonioni there is no given, self-evident "reality" that speaks for itself once recorded. A modernist and formalist, Antonioni is interested in the real from another perspective—he discards any notion of the certainty of things and surrenders to the "invisible" and unseen reality, the particularities and tonalities of the surface, texture and materiality of things and that arise in the interaction between things. For those who cannot appreciate his films, it is their own loss. For Antonioni challenges the viewer to go as far as she or he is willing to go, in the offer he presents of a new experience and way of seeing. He will always remain a brilliant and significant director for the way he pushed narrative fiction into what Deleuze has called "the void."[3]

Zabriskie Point came after the significant body of work Antonioni made throughout the '50s and '60s, and was his first film set in America. The story takes its cue from the hotbed of political unrest prevalent on university campuses at the time (late '60s) and the conflict between the counter culture and the "establishment". From the film's first shot, we're plunged into a room flooded with faces and voices in what reveals itself to be a student meeting. With '70s Afro lingo and in typical student style, the students debate and discuss what it is to be a revolutionary, the importance of recognising the enemy and the tactics and course of action to take. Several scenes on and we see a bloody confrontation between the students and the police.

Antonioni doesn't tell us what specifically they're fighting for, he doesn't dramatise the conflict at all, but it is clear who he sides with. The police are revealed to be merciless and unjustifiably violent in their actions toward the students. In fact, all the characters who represent the "establishment" in this film, from the heartless police to the men and women who work in corporate America, are revealed in a fairly one-dimensional way as money driven and shallow. Antonioni revels in the "gags" that the students in their counter cultural sensibility play: answering the phone with "goodbye", searching for the "fantastic" place for meditation, giving one's name as "Karl Marx", and so on.

That Antonioni privileges the values of the counter culture over the "establishment" is further illustrated in the way he frames the urban landscape as a space dominated and bombarded by advertising billboards that dwarf the inhabitants of the city. Like the billboard that apes a farm landscape, this "reality" of consumerism reflected in the overwhelming billboards, is mistaken as the given reality—

and, of course, Antonioni's intentions are to reveal a brighter, sunnier and utopic alternative. It is the students, with their spiritual openness and soul-searching motives who become the proponents of his deep concerns and vision, and lead the viewer to this world.

The oppositions operating in *Zabriskie Point* are a little over-simplified and reductionist. If there is a flaw in this film, it lies here. But maybe it's too easy to make such a claim in retrospect. Regardless, Antonioni draws this schema only to dismiss it and push the narrative into other spaces. Yet he doesn't dismiss these oppositions entirely, he taps into the values of the "hippy culture" and celebrates them in the gesture he makes in returning to nature as utopia, the mythic ideal, and "true" reality.

NOTES

1 Sam Rohdie, *Antonioni*, BFI, London, 1990, p. 3.

2 A thesis that underlies his book *Antonioni*.

3 Gilles Deleuze, *Cinema 1—the movement-image*, University of Minnesota Press, Minneapolis, 1986, p. 120.

—Fiona A. Villella, "Here Comes the Sun: New Ways of Seeing in Antonioni's *Zabriskie Point*," in Senses of Cinema, issue no. 4 [online journal]. Melbourne, Australia [cited March 2000]; available from www.sensesofcinema.com. INTERNET.

Buried Child

Buried Child was first produced at the Magic Theatre in San Francisco, where Shepard was playwright in residence from 1974-1984. It won the Pulitzer Prize in 1979. *Buried Child* reflects Shepard's preoccupation with the American frontier myth, and it introduces a theme of incest that has reverberations in his later work. In this play, the mythic old west, with its muscularity and rambling adventurousness, is merely a dream; what replaces it is an eerily isolated farmhouse and a family whose dark secret has made them monsters and contaminants to anyone who dares enter. Critics have tended to place this play—with its unearthed corpse, haunting secret, and dilapidated house—in the genre of "frontier gothic" alongside writers like Edgar Allan Poe and William Faulkner. In addition, *Buried Child* has been placed in the company of Eugene O'Neill's, Tennessee Williams' and Arthur Miller's family dramas.

As Act One begins, we are in the living room of an old isolated farmhouse where Dodge, a decrepit man in his seventies with a chronic cough, sits in front of a silent TV drinking whiskey from a bottle that has been carefully concealed in the tattered couch. He bickers with the disembodied voice of his wife Halie as it carries down to him from a room upstairs. They engage in a drawn out dispute in which Halie nags and wheedles from upstairs and Dodge, between coughs and swigs from the bottle, snaps back defensively about his health, his unwillingness to let their son Bradley give him a haircut, and some unnamed man from Halie's past.

At Dodge's loud beckoning, his oldest son Tilden enters the room. He is in his late forties and as stage directions indicate, "Something about him is profoundly burned out and displaced." Tilden, having had some "trouble" in New Mexico, is now, after an absence of twenty years, staying with Dodge and Halie. He brings an armful of corn he claims came suddenly from their backyard, which has been barren for many years. Tilden husks the corn in front of Dodge while Halie, still from upstairs, reveals the family history —how Tilden, an All-American fullback, was too much trouble; Bradley, her next son, was stupid enough to chop his own leg off with a chain saw; and Ansel, the smartest and most promising of them all, died mysteriously on his honeymoon and "left us all alone." Critics are somewhat divided on the symbolic significance of Tilden's husking corn in the midst of Halie's bleak revelations. Some call the corn husking surreal and nonsensical, while others see the corn as a representation of fertility and life that stands ironically out of place in the wasteland surrounding it.

Halie descends finally from upstairs, wearing a black mourning dress. Seeing the corn all over the room, Halie expresses her utter disgust at the thieving Tilden and her "decomposing" and "putrid" husband, meanwhile berating Dodge for speaking against their other son Bradley. To counter her absurd nitpicking, Dodge tells her that his flesh and blood is buried in the backyard, which at last brings a long pause to the mudslinging. Halie leaves to have lunch with the minister, Father Dewis. Dodge, thrown into a coughing attack at the prospect of being left alone when Bradley arrives, takes a pill and falls asleep. As Dodge is sleeping Tilden steals his bottle of whiskey, covers him with cornhusks and leaves. Bradley enters, knocking his wooden leg clumsily around. After roughly moving away the cornhusks and jerking off Dodge's cap, he begins shaving his father's hair with electric clippers as he sleeps. Bradley's savage treatment of his father is one of the many moments in Shepard's work where the archetypal relationship between father and son, with all its pain and uncertainty, is foisted on the audience with brutal clarity.

Act Two begins that evening. Dodge still sleeps, now with his hair cut so short that his scalp bleeds in some places. Vince, Tilden's twenty-two year old son, enters with his girlfriend, Shelly, who laughs it off as a Norman Rockwell house. Dodge wakes up when Shelly touches one of his cuts, and the young couple become disturbed to find that Dodge does not recognize his grandson after a mere six years. In this scene, Shelly's initial impression of the house proves to be absolutely off the mark: Dodge, with bleeding head, tears out the stuffing of the couch in search of his liquor bottle, Tilden refers to a son that was buried in the backyard, and then Dodge begins to wheedle Vince about going out and buying him another bottle. Vince, now dejected at the family's refusal of his identity, finally agrees to go get Dodge his bottle and insists Shelly stay. Here Shepard shows the dark side of the frontier myth—Vince has gone from being happily transient to eerily rootless.

After Vince leaves, Dodge admits to Shelly that he recognizes a face inside Vince's face. Tilden reveals to Shelly that Halie had a baby that Dodge drowned and then buried in the backyard. Ironically it takes Tilden, the character described by his mother as "not in control of his faculties," to bring the family out of its insane indifference to the origin of their pain. By this time Dodge has coughed so hard he has fallen on the floor. Bradley enters, taunting Tilden and Dodge for having once been All American athletes and ending up lazy and wasting away. To Shelly he suggests shooting or drowning Dodge. Then he forces Shelly to hold her mouth open while he puts his fingers in and holds them there. In keeping with the gothic tradition, the deeper one delves into this mysterious house and its occupants, the more frightening and sadistic it appears.

The following morning, (Act Three), Vince and Halie are still gone, and Shelly has slept in Halie's room. Bradley is asleep on the sofa under Dodge's blanket and his leg is propped up next to him. Dodge leans against the TV using Shelly's coat as a blanket. Halie, now in a bright yellow dress and slightly drunk, enters with Father Dewis. She becomes irritably ashamed at the poor impression her family makes, and swiftly pulls the coat off Dodge, covers Bradley's leg with it, then pulls the blanket off Bradley and throws it on Dodge. A helpless Bradley whines angrily for his blanket, only to be chided by his mother like a child. Halie, who claims the house has a stench of sin, is aloof to Shelly, and instead kicks Dodge for losing track of Tilden. The cacophony rises as Bradley and Dodge fight over the blanket, and finally Shelly, enraged about being ignored, shatters a cup and saucer against the door. Shelly takes Bradley's leg hostage as she forces the family to talk about their secret. Dodge explains that the family was well established until Halie mysteriously got pregnant well after she and Dodge had stopped sleeping in the same room. The child, beloved by Tilden, was seen as an enormous blemish on the family, so Dodge killed it. Here the past incestuous relationship between Halie and Tilden is painfully clear; though some critics point out that Halie's obvious philandering the night before makes equally possible that another man besides Tilden could have been the actual father of her child.

Vince enters, falling on his stomach on the back porch in a drunken stupor. He begins smashing empty bottles against the opposite end of the porch and singing. To Shelly's astonishment, Halie recognizes him. Vince cuts the screen surrounding the porch with his hunting knife. Father Dewis takes Halie upstairs to protect her and Vince enters the house. As Bradley crawls in pursuit of his wooden leg, Vince repeatedly kicks it out of his reach. A dying Dodge proclaims that Vince will inherit the house and continues to speak his last will and testament. Vince tells Shelly he will not leave with her because he has just inherited the house and wants to "carry on the line" and "keep things rolling." He explains that he drove all night, studying his face in the windshield as it rained. He saw the face of his father and forefathers and further, "as far back as they'd take me. Then it all dissolved." This statement refers back to Dodge's observation to Shelly that he recognized a face inside Vince's; here Shepard problematizes the relationship between personal identity and family lineage.

Father Dewis comes from upstairs, asking Vince to help his grandmother, whom Vince denies exists. He simply sits on the sofa and stares at a newly deceased Dodge. Halie shouts down to Dodge from upstairs; meanwhile Tilden returns, muddied from the knees down. He carries the corpse of the lost child wrapped in the original burial cloth. Unaware, Vince stares at the ceiling, while Tilden, eyes fixed to the corpse of the child, walks upstairs. The lights fade as Halie muses from upstairs about a miracle crop that has suddenly popped out of the ground.

Buried Child

Dodge is a sickly old man in his seventies who was once an All American athlete. He is miserably thin and weak, suffers from a chronic racking cough, and spends most of his time under an old blanket on the couch in front of the TV. His one comfort is sneaking drinks of whiskey behind the backs of his screeching and insulting wife, his half-witted son Tilden, and his bullying son Bradley. By his account to Shelly, his misery originated from the unexpected pregnancy of his wife by another man—probably his son Tilden— the offspring of which he killed and buried in the backyard. Dodge continues his retaliation by withholding the secret of where the body is buried. When he finally confesses his secret, he verbally wills his possessions to his family and dies.

Halie is Dodge's wife, aged about 65. She continues to mother her two sons Tilden and Bradley, both of whom are in their forties, as if they were children. She is riddled with rage and disgust over the way her family has turned out—her husband "decomposing on the couch, the farm gone, her two sons utter disgraces to the family." She maintains her tenuous hold on sanity by campaigning to memorialize her long deceased son Ansel, whom she holds up as a hero tragically snuffed out by the Mob. She is fiercely protective of the family secret—her middle aged illegitimate pregnancy and the "disappearance" of its offspring—and is literally faced with it at the end of the play as Tilden brings the unearthed corpse of the baby to her in her bedroom.

Tilden is Dodge's and Halie's oldest son. Reminiscent of Lenny in Steinbeck's *Of Mice and Men*, Tilden is a slightly retarded man in his late forties. A former All American athlete like his father, he has recently returned to live with Halie and Dodge again after disappearing for twenty years. Apparently in trouble with the law for unnamed misdeeds in New Mexico, he cannot be trusted when unsupervised by either Halie or Dodge and tends to wander off and steal produce. When Halie's illegitimate child was born, Tilden cared deeply for it, singing and talking to the baby for hours at a time. Now, encouraged by Shelly, he retells the story of the child and eventually wanders off to find the hidden body in the backyard. As the play ends, Tilden can be seen carrying the decomposed body up the stairs to Halie's room.

Bradley is Dodge's and Halie's next oldest son. He is an amputee, and according to Halie, chopped his leg off with a chain saw. At the beginning of the play, he behaves like a schoolyard bully, stomping around and terrorizing everyone but his mother. Apparently he needs to "turn the tables" on Dodge and Tilden, who he claims once mistreated him, by making them fear him as much as possible. However, when Bradley's wooden leg is unattached, he is defenseless and weak; when Shelly takes his leg and Vince kicks it out of his reach, Bradley's bravado disappears, and he becomes a whining, oversized boy.

Vince, in his early twenties, is Tilden's son and Dodge's and Halie's grandson. He has not seen his family in six years and stops by the house to visit his grandparents on the way to see his father in New Mexico. Unaware of the fact that Tilden has returned and that his family is disturbed, he is dismayed to find that Tilden and Dodge do not recognize him and mistreat both him and his girlfriend Shelly. What starts out as an innocent trip through his past becomes a nightmare of failed recognition and shocking dysfunction. While out to buy Dodge a bottle of whiskey, he instead takes an all-night drive in the rain, in which he has a vision of his forebears in the reflection of his visage in the windshield. Returning to the house in a drunken stupor, he decides to claim the house as his inheritance and, unaware of Dodge's dead body and the baby's corpse in Tilden's hand, he sinks eerily into the couch and into the role of the men that came before him.

Shelly is Vince's girlfriend and traveling companion. A city girl from L.A., stylishly dressed, she is out of her element in this farmhouse. At first she finds the place hilarious, but when she sees that Vince's father and grandfather don't recognize him, suffers the torture of Vince's uncle Bradley, and sees how the place has a perverse hold on her boyfriend, she is horrified. Nevertheless, her own perversity causes her to stay overnight in Halie's bedroom, emerge with a sense that the house is really hers, and play the role of Dodge's caretaker. It is when she feels she is being ignored, especially by Halie, that she shows her ability to both take control and spin the bizarre events into more chaos. She shatters a cup and saucer, takes Bradley's leg hostage, and insists the family stop pretending there is no hideous secret. Her unease with their denial ultimately jolts the family into seeing who they are; Dodge tells the story of the buried child, Tilden goes to dig it up, and Halie, Vince and Bradley choose to spin more fantasies. As such, Shelly fulfils her dramatic purpose and leaves.

Father Dewis is a protestant minister and companion of Halie. He humors her desire to memorialize her son Ansel with a large statue by ostensibly bringing her cause to the City Council. Halie leaves for a lunch appointment with him and they both return to the house the following day, drunk. Father Dewis, supposedly coming in the house for tea, is disoriented by the family crisis that ensues when Halie begins to question what has happened in her absence. He is caught in the middle as Halie complains to him of the putrid stench of sin in her house. Finally, after Dodge tells the story of the dead child, Father Dewis helps Halie upstairs and takes a genuine interest in her welfare, though he admits to Vince that he is utterly unable to help in any significant way.

CRITICAL VIEWS ON

Buried Child

RICHARD EDER ON THE PLAY AS A LAMENTATION OF A LOST
AMERICAN IDEAL

[Richard Eder writes book reviews and articles for *The New
York Times*. In this excerpt, Eder argues that beneath
Shepard's derogatory portrayal of the American family lies
a sincere lament of the loss of an ideal.]

Sam Shepard structure does not merely denounce chaos and anomie
in American life, he mourns over them. His corrosive images and
scenes of absurdity never soften to concede the presence of a lament,
but it is there all the same.

Denunciation that has no pity in it is pamphleteering at best and
a striking of fashionable attitudes at worst, and it is fairly common
on the contemporary stage. Mr. Shepard is an uncommon playwright
and uncommonly gifted and he does not take denouncing for
granted. He wrestles with it at the risk of being thrown.

Recently he has been writing about families. "Curse of the
Starving Class" used the image of physical hunger as a symbol of
moral starvation. It was a fierce, funny, unmanageable play whose
imagery never quite worked.

"Buried Child", now at the Theater for the New City, takes the
same theme. As a piece of writing, it may be less interesting but it
seems to work far better on the stage. In the very gifted production
directed by Robert Woodruff, it manages to be vividly alive even as
it is putting together a surreal presentation of American intimacy
withered by rootlessness.

It takes the form of a homecoming. Vince, who has been away for
six years, comes home bringing his saxophone and his Los Angeles
girlfriend. Home is an Illinois farm where his grandparents live. It
was flourishing once and he comes with the most bucolic memories
and a determination to get to know his family and his roots.

What he finds is a house of the dying, full of grotesques clinging to
guilty secrets. His grandmother preaches morality and goes out on

all-night bashes with the local clergyman. His grandfather is a bitter, self-absorbed drunk who, as it turns out, has murdered an unwanted child. Vince's father, Tilden, is half-crazed; he keeps bringing in armloads of corn and carrots that grow even though nobody has planted them. Finally, there is a brutal uncle who has lost a leg to a chain saw.

It is a far cry from the apple pie, turkey, and kindly old relatives that Shelly, the girl, has been told to expect. By the time the visit is over she has been insulted, assaulted, set to peel Tilden's supernatural carrots, and generally abused. Vince, who had thought of the visit as a voyage through memory, fares even worse. His memories don't remember him. His relatives ignore him or send him out to buy whisky.

Dodge, the fierce, dying grandfather who is the shattered heart of this American household, has no use for progeny or for any future.

"You're all alike, you hopers," he tells Shelly, and clings to his whisky, his television and a battered baseball cap. The future is meaningless to him and the past is even more meaningless. "I'm descended from a long line of corpses," he says, "and there's not a living soul behind me." Shepard's America has poisoned its roots and destroyed its life.

> —Richard Eder, "Stage: Sam Shepard Offers 'Buried Child,'" *The New York Times*, 7 November 1978. *The New York Theatre Critics' Reviews* (1978): 146.

MEL GUSSOW ON THE PLAY'S CENTRAL THEME OF RECOGNITION AND IDENTITY

[Mel Gussow is a drama critic for the *New York Times* and the author of *Conversations With Pinter* (1994), *Conversations With Stoppard* (1995), and *Edward Albee: A Singular Journey: A Biography* (1999). In this excerpt, Gussow shows that each of the play's characters searches for a lost identity.]

One of the many themes in Sam Shepard's tantalizing play "Buried Child" (in a new production at the Yale Repertory Theater) is the question of recognition and identity. How do we know who—and what—we are? In the play, which is also running Off Broadway, a prodigal grandson returns to the family homestead after an absence of six years, and no one knows him, or, perhaps, everyone pretends not to know him.

Finally, his father peers into his eyes and thinks that he recognizes "the face within the face." This phrase refers to the child within the man, the past behind the present, and also the father himself. For a moment, he thinks that in his son he sees his own image.

Each of the strange characters in "Buried Child" is searching for his heritage, as if it were something that had been mislaid in the attic or under the derelict sofa. The grizzled old grandfather, Dodge, traces his roots back to the grave, and, as we watch him, he appear's to be disintegrating into dust.

The symbol of this mordant clan—the American family gone to seed—is the buried child of the title, an infant who has mysteriously disappeared. In the play, we see three lost generations of one family. The grandfather has been replaced; he lingers without purpose, cauterizing himself with alcohol and television. His older son has misplaced his reason; he is unable to function in an adult society. The grandson is displaced; where does he belong?

The tone of the play is almost surrealistic. Like a figure out of Ionesco, the father brings in armloads of fresh vegetables from a garden that has been barren for years. As Dodge waspishly comments, "Can you trust a man who keeps bringing in vegetables from out of nowhere?"

To those unfamiliar with the work of Mr. Shepard, the play itself may seem to be coming "from out of nowhere." Actually it has its roots firmly in America, and in our concept of the family as an ideal. "Buried Child" is one of Mr. Shepard's most accessible works, principally because we view this family through the eyes of an impressionable outsider, a young woman accompanying the grandson on a journey into his past. She expects to find "apple pie and turkey dinner." Instead, she discovers cynicism, infantilism and hints of brutality.

This may not sound like a comedy but it is funny, particularly the second of the three acts, when the young woman is suddenly beset by a kitchen closet of family skeletons. Adrian Hall's Yale production is more overtly amusing than Robert Woodruff's current Off Broadway production of the play, but in the end it is no less serious. (...)

As the visitor, Polly Draper, a student at the Yale School of Drama, has the necessary combination of tentativeness and boldness. She is alternately repelled and amused by this unseemly household.

The son—and vegetable bearer—in the Yale production is a much more child-like creature than the character that we saw Off Broadway. John Seitz portrays him almost as if he were the backward Lennie in "Of Mice and Men"—with a gentleness that belies his hulking appearance. In contrast, the grandson (Tony Shalhoub) becomes a more defiant character.

Finally, the difference in the two productions is one of gradation rather than of interpretation. Despite somewhat different approaches, both end at the same destination—a dirge for the decline of traditional values, a wake for the American dream. "Buried Child," a penetrating excavation into the essence of blood ties, is further proof that Mr. Shepard is, in several senses, one of our most prodigious dramatists.

> —Mel Gussow, "Prodigal Grandson," *New York Times*, 25 January 1979. *New York Times Theater Reviews* (1979-80): 15.

LYNDA HART ON THE PLAY'S BLEND OF REALISM AND SURREALISM

[Lynda Hart is the author of *Fatal Women: Lesbian Sexuality and the Mark of Aggression* (1994) and *Between the Body and Flesh: Performing Sadomasochism* (1998) and the editor of and *Making a Spectacle: Feminist Essays on Contemporary Women's Theatre* (1989) and *Of All the Nerve: Deb Margolin, Solo* (1999). In this excerpt, Hart inquires into the realism of the play, calling it neither naturalistic nor surreal but a convergence of the two.]

In Shepard's next play, *Buried Child* (1978), he continues to focus on father and son relationships, this time examining three generations in a single family. Again Shepard works within an essentially naturalistic framework; but this play comes close to mocking the form. Jack Richardson comments on the peculiar blending of forms that Shepard achieves:

> Somehow, Shepard manages to strike a balance between naturalistic detail and the wilder, more secret landscapes of being. He has found a way of maintaining a tension between the banal and the strange that gives his plays the quality of lucid dreams.[11]

Nowhere in the playwright's work is this convergence more apparent than in the Pulitzer prize-winning *Buried Child*, a play that on the surface appears wholly naturalistic, conceding to Zola's demand for "direct observation, accurate anatomy, acceptance and representation of what *exists*."[12] Shepard's play carefully sustains a realistic veneer, adhering almost formulaically to the familiar Ibsen/Strindberg brand of realism in theme and structure. The device of a fatal secret deeply hidden beneath the surface of a mundane domestic scene is gradually revealed through dialogue and action, the revelation resulting in a profound conflict that threatens permanent disruption of the normality and tranquility of the domestic life of the family. As the catastrophe approaches, weighty significance is retrospectively attached to words and behavior that originally appeared without import. Dramatic irony magnifies the action of the drama as a final transvaluation, a moral and psychological upheaval, forever alters the perception and consciousness of characters and audience. In this familiar dramatic form, the structure of the plot is essentially a puzzle with each character in custody of clues that are part of the total picture, a picture that begins fragmented but will cohere as the action unfolds, forming a conceptually satisfying unity.

Ibsen may leave his characters and audience with an unresolved moral dilemma or with perplexing psychological ambiguities, but basic questions concerning the nature of past actions, and the identity and relationship of characters are revealed through an exchange of information. On the other hand, although in *Buried Child* Shepard intentionally sets up an audience to follow the tantalizing clues that he exhibits in an effort to integrate the fragments into an accommodating whole, he undercuts our expectations, frustrating our ability to resolve the action of the play realistically, allegorically, *or* symbolically. (...)

Despite the virtually incomprehensible behavior of Dodge and Tilden, we are still encouraged to search for realistic explanations as we respond to Vince's determined effort to force their recognition. Vince can scarcely allow that his physical appearance has changed so drastically in six years as to render him unrecognizable, but in desperation he admits the possibility and begins performing tricks that he entertained them with as a child, hoping that his youthful games will jar their memories. His tricks eliciting no response, Vince sarcastically suggests that perhaps he has committed some moral offense such as "plung[ing] into sinful infatuation with the Alto Saxophone" that may have caused his family to reject him (p. 97). Vince thus posits two reasons, one physical, one moral, in a last attempt to alleviate his confusion and resulting distress. Both attempts fail, and Shelly, embarrassed by her boyfriend's pathetic behavior, admonishes him: "Jesus Christ. They're not gonna play. Can't you see that?" (p. 96). Shelly's comment reopens the possibility that Dodge and Tilden are in collusion, sharing an understanding somehow connected to the secret they share, and Vince is an innocent victim of some sinister intent. We are still, however, unable to discover a reason for the game; indeed, the search for one will prove futile. Perhaps it is at this point in the play's action that we should abandon the search, for after all it appears that the realistic surface of the drama has been irreparably cracked. (...)

The ostensibly realistic structure is thus a perversion of naturalistic convention, an uncommon form in the American theatre, but following the pattern Schechner describes as essentially Pinteresque, "conceptual incompleteness, the conceptual world out of which the plays emerge ... sparse, fragmented ... no single rational frame to answer all the questions."[17] As in Pinter's plays, we never know why certain actions occur in *Buried Child*, and we are not meant to know. No intelligible pattern is disclosed behind the dissociated actions, confounding Zola's scientific method of observation, in itself far from an avant-garde stance since a whole movement in modern drama, beginning perhaps with Ibsen's *The*

Master Builder, has been away from the belief in logical causality and the capacity for objectivity. But Shepard's play strikes us as radically different because of the convergence of the naturalistic form, cognitive and realistic, with disturbing action that exactly reverses an audience's expectations. Motives are left undiscovered; the past is revealed but fails to illuminate the present; character becomes increasingly disorganized and action unpredictable. The two antithetical forms jarringly combine to produce an uneasy, inexplicable action that taunts our ability to make our observations intelligible.

NOTES

[11]Jack Richardson, introduction, Buried Child, Seduced, and Suicide in B^b (New York: Urizen Books, 1979), ii.

[12] Emile Zola, The Experimental Novel and other Essays, trans. Belle M. Sherman (New York: Cassell Pub., 1983), reprinted in Bernard F. Dukore, ed., Dramatic Theory and Criticism (New York: Holt, Rinehart, and Winston, Inc., 1974) pp. 695-696

[17] Richard Schechner, "Puzzling Pinter," *The Tulane Drama Review*, 11, No. 2 (Winter, 1966), 176–185.

> —Lynda Hart, *Sam Shepard's Metaphorical Stages*, (New York: Greenwood Press, 1987): 75-76, 79-80, 81-82.

DORIS AUERBACH ON THE POWERLESS MOTHER FIGURE IN THE PLAY

[Doris Auerbach is the author of *Sam Shepard, Arthur Kopit, and the Off BroadwayTheater* (1982). In this excerpt, Auerbach argues that Halie, like many of the mother figures that appear in Shepard's plays, is weak and ineffectual in protecting the family from the father's cruel dominance.]

From the mother, lying ill in bed in *Rock Garden*, one of his earliest plays, to the two flaky mothers in *A Lie of the Mind*, his latest, Sam Shepard has created a series of mother figures who are too weak to counteract the violence of the fathers. They lack the will and the power to restore order in their world, to bring about a family in balance, one that can nurture its children.

Shepard has used as his paradigm for the family in crisis, the overwhelming cultural myth of the American West. He portrays an eternal battle between the women gatherers who settle down, grow food and create civilization, and men, the nomadic hunters, who survive by violence and flee the ties of family and commitment. (...)

In his epitaph on the American family as an institution and the decay of the American dream, *Buried Child* (1978), Shepard exposes the skeleton in the American family closet—the theme of incest which reemerges in all his major plays to follow. Shepard, has always been noted for his skillful use of archetypal myths. As early as 1969 in *The Holy Ghostly* he introduced the eternal struggle between father and son. There is no mention of a mother figure in that early play, only the cowboy son returning home to confront the father and wrest power from him. In Shepard's depiction of the American West, the cowboy is the violent, isolated victor who flees from civilization and defeats the attempts of the mother to create a nurturing family. In *Buried Child*, however, Shepard reveals the struggle of the father to keep his son from gaining power. As I have noted elsewhere, Dodge, the father who has always 'dodged' responsibility for his sons, is a threatening father whose infanticidal impulse still haunts him and creates unconscious guilt in the audience. The powerless mother figure is not only unable to protect her children but has the violence of the father projected onto her: "You never saw a bitch eating her puppies?" (*Buried Child* 54). Like Weston in *Curse*, Dodge sees paternity only as a phallic exercise of potency. He rejects caring for his children, for, like Cronus, he fears death at the hands of his progeny.

The farm, like the family, has grown barren; only Tilden, the profoundly burnt-out son, believes the fertile paradise he vaguely remembers can be restored again. Tilden is one of the defenseless males who is aligned with the equally powerless mothers against the fathers' world of power, dominance and violence. Tilden, the tiller of the soil, wanted to create the son who would make the land fruitful again, the son who would be strong enough to turn his back on the world of the fathers, who would create a new world which would end patriarchy's violent hegemony. This was the child he conceived with his mother, Halie, who like Eve, bore the child in pain, the child that "begged" to be born (Auerbach 60). This was the child that Tilden nurtured: "he'd walk all night out in the pasture with it. Talkin' to it. Singing to it. Used to hear him singing to it" (*Buried Child* 65). This was the child that threatened Dodge's patriarchal power and was killed by him. The mother and the nurturing procreator, Tilden, were unable to protect it. Dodge commits infanticide: "Couldn't allow a thing like that to grow up in the middle of our lives" (*Buried Child* 61). The existence of this child, conceived through incest, would destroy the violent world of the father. But how else are new worlds founded?—With whom did Adam's son mate but with Eve? The play ends like a miracle play with the symbol of the resurrection. The child is taken from the tomb, tended by Tilden and carried up, not to the patriarchal figure who lies dead on stage before us but to the mother who is waiting above.

—Doris Auerbach, "Who Was Icarus' Mother? The Powerless Mother Figures in the Plays of Sam Shepard." *Sam Shepard: A Casebook*, ed. Kimball King (New York: Garland Publishing, Inc., 1988): 53-54, 56-57.

DAVID J. DEROSE ON THE PLAY'S UNFIXING OF REALITY

[David J. DeRose's essays on Sam Shepard have appeared in *Theater, American Theatre,* and *Theatre Journal.* In this excerpt, DeRose argues that Shepard begins the play with a surface realism only to shatter it later.]

Curse of the Starving Class's final metaphoric image of the members of the family as cat and eagle caught in a mutually destructive embrace is reimagined in *Buried Child*. Here, the family is a black hole that holds its offspring in a deadly grip, eventually sucking them back into its vortex. Vince, who has not seen his family in six years, has returned to his grandparents' farmhouse in Illinois. Like Oswald in Ibsen's *Ghosts*, he has been living the "debauched" life of the artist in the big city, and he has undertaken a journey toward what he thought was home to seek out his father and to face his personal ghosts. His girlfriend, Shelly, tells us that he has stopped in "every stupid little donut shop he ever kissed a girl in"[9] searching for his heritage. Shelly, who expected Vince's family to be something out of a Norman Rockwell illustration with "turkey dinners and apple pie and all that kinda stuff," is confronted by a radically different vision that, in one critic's words, is "as if Grant Wood's American Gothic family were perceived while on a bad acid trip."[10]

When Vince arrives at his grandparents' house, neither his father, Tilden, nor his grandfather, Dodge, claims to remember him. The only child missing from the family as far as they are concerned is the one buried in the backyard. Tilden and Dodge are just two of the emotional and physical cripples who inhabit the once-flourishing household. Dodge cannot, or will not, move from the sofa where he sits wrapped in a blanket, taking guarded sips from the whiskey bottle he has hidden under the cushions. Tilden, who has recently returned after years of living alone in the desert, is more like a gigantic child, his brain numbed by too much sun and alcohol.

Vince's arrival marks the near-completion of a cycle that began more than 30 years earlier. He is the last of the men in his family to return to his grandparents' house, to be drawn into the vortex of communal family secrets that has given birth to this crippled brood and that seems to be a final resting place for the family's men. Among those men are Vince's deranged uncle, Bradley (who cut his leg off in a chain-saw accident), his dead uncle, Ansel (who mysteriously perished on his honeymoon), and the buried child of the play's title.

The house's only female inhabitant is Dodge's wife, Halie. The play begins with the sound of Halie's disembodied voice coming from her bedroom upstairs, where she watches the rain come down "in sheets" outside her window while Dodge sits downstairs staring at a blank television screen. Both Halie and Dodge inhabit worlds of their own creation. Permanently rooted to his sofa, Dodge isolates himself from the outside world, trying to hide from and forget his family and his past. Halie, meanwhile, surrounds herself with pictures of the past and of her family in its prime. Early in the play, she leaves the house to meet with a local pastor, Father Dewis, in order to re-create the past and repopulate her world with heroes to replace the monsters to which she has given birth.

Rather than create the kind of immediately disorienting stage image and action he used in *Curse of the Starving Class*, throwing the audience into turmoil before it had the opportunity to settle into the rhythm of the play, Shepard applies a stage aesthetic in *Buried Child* akin to that he used in one of his earliest plays, *Icarus's Mother*. In that play, the action began in a relatively realistic manner and only gradually came unfixed.

The lesson had been, as director Michael Smith noted, that the play "needs reality in order to transcend reality" (Smith, *Notes*, 28). *Buried Child* opens upon what appears to be a conventional realistic situation within a traditional domestic setting: Dodge watching television in the front room of his Illinois farmhouse. An old wooden staircase with frayed carpet leads "offstage left up into the wings with no landing." Dodge sits on a dark green sofa "with the stuffing coming out in spots," facing the television with the "blue light flickering on his face." Behind the sofa is a large, screened-in porch with a screen door "leading from the porch to the outside. Beyond that are the shapes of dark elm trees" (*BC*, 63).

Since writing *Buried Child*, Shepard has acknowledged that he can unfix stage reality more effectively by starting a dramatic action with a surface realism that places the audience (falsely) at ease: "I like to set it up at the beginning so that everybody's happy, so that nobody's trying to figure anything out. Everything's okay to begin with. To begin with something that is immediately unrecognizable [,too] immediately mysterious is confusing, because no one knows where to go. But if everybody starts out thinking they know where they're going, *then* you can go in a different direction. *Then* you can go off into territory unknown" (Lippman, 15). In *Buried Child*, this principle is achieved both through the seemingly ordinary stage setting and through the presence of Dodge, a likable old Curmudgeon, whose wry humor and mocking disdain for Halie's attempts at dialogue quickly disarm the audience.

NOTES

[9] *Buried Child* in *Seven Plays* (New York: Bantam Books, 1981), 119; hereafter cited in text as *BC*.

[10] Bernard Weiner, "Sam Shepard's 'Buried Child'—A Major, Bitter New Play," *San Francisco Chronicle*, 6 August 1978, 19.

—David J. DeRose, *Sam Shepard*, (New York: Twayne Publishers, 1992): 99-101.

ANN WILSON ON CORRESPONDENCES BETWEEN THE PLAY
AND SHEPARD'S MEMOIRS

[Ann Wilson is the editor of *Howard Brenton: A Casebook*
(1992) and *Prerogatives: Contemporary Plays by Women*
(1998). In this excerpt, Wilson compares the character of
Dodge to Shepard's description of his own grandfather in
his book *Motel Chronicles* (1982).]

Buried Child, on its simplest level, is an exploration of identity. The
strangeness of the family in *Buried Child* makes it difficult to
imagine that Shepard might be exploring his own family. Yet the
autobiographic component of *Buried Child* is suggested by the
correspondences between the play and a piece in *Motel Chronicles*,
a collection of poems, prose, reflections and photographs which are
Shepard's recollection of his own life—or so we are told on the
book's jacket. In this piece, Shepard writes about visiting his
grandparents who lived near Chicago:

> My grandfather sits as he's always sat—in a hole of his sofa
> wrapped in crocheted blankets facing the T.V. He's like a skeleton
> now... He smokes and drinks continuously and spits blood into a
> stand-up brass ashtray like you see in lobbies of old hotels.
> Sometimes he coughs so violently his whole body doubles over
> and he can't catch his breath for a long time. His world is cir-
> cumscribed around the sofa. Everything he needs is within a
> three-foot reach. The T.V. is only on for the baseball. When the
> game ends my Grandmother comes in and turns it off. She does it
> right on cue. She can hear when the game ends from any room in
> the house. She has great ears.
>
> When everyone's asleep I wander around in the room
> upstairs staring at all the photographs of my Uncles. The Uncle
> who dies in a motel room on his wedding night. His wife who
> died with him. The Uncle who lost a leg at the age of ten. The
> Uncle who married into the Chicago Mafia... All the Uncles who
> carry the bones of my Grandpa's face.[22]

Certainly Dodge and Halie are recognisable in Shepard's
description of his grandparents while Bradley and Ansel (who
married into the 'Mob') seem similar to Shepard's description of his
uncles. Shepard's nocturnal viewing of the family photographs

reminds us of Shelly who goes upstairs at night and looks at the photographs of the family which are hanging on the wall. The comment that the uncles carry the bones of their father in their faces is developed fully in Vince's speech about his vision of the family, which comes to him as a reflection in the windshield of the car as he drives towards the Iowa border (130). These correspondences create links between the two works and, at the same time, call into question the status of *Motel Chronicles*: is it document or fiction?

Shepard, in his interview with Kevin Sessums, is clear about the status of *Motel Chronicles* as a work of fiction. When asked by Sessums whether he will write a novel, Shepard replies, 'Oh man, I've tried it and tried it. The only serious attempt I really made, I guess, was with *Motel Chronicles* but it just broke into a million pieces. A novel just seems beyond me'.[23] Yet despite Shepard's claim that *Motel Chronicles* is fiction, it reads like a series of his notes on, and recollections of, his life. Many of the pieces, particularly those recounting specific moments with his family, seem extremely intimate, and hence authentic, because ours is a culture which equates the dropping of the public persona with the revelation of the private, real, and therefore, authentic, self.

The veracity of the pieces in *Motel Chronicles* is not simply reinforced by the use of photographs but depends on it. Most of the photographs show Shepard with his family and indeed, the volume is a sort of family album. The use of these photographs is more complicated than simply being illustrative because they direct us to read the written text in a particular way. Photographs, Roland Barthes informs us, record 'the scene itself, the literal reality. From the object to its image, there is of course a reduction: in proportion, in perspective, in colour. But this reduction is at no point a *transformation* ...'[24] In other words, what a photograph creates is an apparently unproblematic relation between the object and its image because the photograph is a record, unmediated by the photographer's selection of elements in the scene. In contrast to a painting in which the painter selects what is to be included in the work, the photograph records whatever is in range of the lens. In short, a photograph is supposedly a record of reality, not a rendering.

Because *Motel Chronicles* is composed of photos, poems and bits of prose, an intertextual network is established within the volume itself: photographs and writing are read in relation to one another.

The proximity of the photograph (which seems artless) to writing, which we normally consider to be artifice because of the mediation of the writer, creates a spill-effect so that writing, read in the context of the photograph, becomes similarly artless—or at least less artful. In the words of Roland Barthes, language is 'made innocent' by its proximity to the photograph. The authenticity of Shepard's apparently intimate revelations about his family is reinforced by the inclusion of the photographic record of family. Both seem to be the true, unmediated representation of reality.

And yet, are they? Several of the photographs, including the shot on the cover, are clearly posed. In the cover photograph, for example, Shepard stands next to a car with Texas license plates. All the clothing he wears is black: pants, t-shirt, jacket and stetson. He holds a bottle of Coca-Cola. In the background is what looks to be a country store, complete with a porch. This portrait creates a persona for Shepard as the dark figure on the landscape of mythic America, metonymically marked by Coca-Cola, cars and cowboys. The scene seems staged, the photograph designed to create a particular effect: the mythologising of Sam Shepard. Yet, as staged as the scene is, it does seem to allude to the actual world: the license plates on the car permit the vehicle to be driven on public roads. The car, the Coke, the clothing, and general store, while serving as props, also have use (and hence value) outside the staged scene. As James Lingwood notes, the 'mythologies photography serve to create cannot easily be separated from our knowledge that it is working with reality'.[25] This tension between the actual and the fictional is an important component of *Buried Child*.

NOTES

[22] Sam Shepard, *Motel Chronicles* (San Francisco: City Lights, 1982), pp. 45, 46.

[23] Sessums, 78.

[24] Roland Barthes, *Camera Lucida: Reflections of Photography*, trans. Richard Howard (New York: Hill and Wang, 1981) p. 5.

[25] James Lingwood, 'Self-Portraits' in *Identity: The Real Me, ICA Documents* 6, ed. Lisa Appisanesi (London: Institute of Contemporary Art, 1987) p. 20.

—Ann Wilson, "True Stories: Reading the Autobiographic in *Cowboy Mouth*, 'True Dylan' and *Buried Child*." *Rereading Shepard: Contemporary Critical Essays on the Plays of Sam Shepard*, ed. Leonard Wilcox (New York: St. Martin's Press, 1993): 108-111.

[Ann C. Hall is the Editor of *Delights, Desires, and
Dilemmas:Essays on Women and the Media* (1998). She has
published articles on Eugene O'Neill, Harold Pinter, and
David Mamet, and several of her original plays have been
published and produced. In this excerpt, Hall argues that
Halie and Shelly are inescapably bound by the "male
economy" of the play.]

With *Buried Child* (1979), Shepard creates a contemporary
American "homecoming," another "long day's journey into night."
As in O'Neill's play, in Shepard's play a family secret is explored
and finally exposed. And as in both O'Neill's and Pinter's plays, a
woman disrupts the familial equilibrium. While Shepard is very
concerned with the question of male violence, in *Buried Child*, he
also explores the nature of paternity. In the end, *Buried Child*
demonstrates that the law of the father is oppressive and that the
family it creates is dysfunctional and violent. The men in the play
are clearly linked to the darker aspects of human behavior. Dodge,
the patriarch, attempts to control the workings of the house from the
living room sofa, but he is old, feeble, and impotent. If we miss the
imagery, his wife, Halie, who is dressed in mourning at the
beginning of the play, frequently refers to him as a corpse. The two
sons, Tilden and Bradley, are not characterized very differently: one
is a half-wit and the other is a menace with a wooden leg. The
disparity between the people and the lush vegetables Tilden brings
home is clear. Shepard's imagery is unmistakable; this middle-class
home is the house of the dead.

And yet, throughout the play, the characters cling to this male
wasteland, its forms and its laws. Even the female character, Halie,
is entangled in patriarchal expectations. She is clearly dissatisfied
with her relationship to Dodge at the beginning of the play, but
rather than attempting to change her relationship to men in general,
she transfers her affections to other men, first to her son Ansel and
then to a "father of the church" after Ansel's death. While she may
not fully participate in the specific workings of her domestic

patriarchy, she is still male-identified, leaving the home to erect monuments in their honor and to search for more suitable male companionship. Despite all the evidence the play presents regarding the patriarchy's impotence, Halie continues to search for a man who will satisfy her.

Her son Vince returns home, hoping to find a sense of himself, but with the mother absent, no one recognizes him. The men have nothing to offer Vince. His female companion, Shelly, also expects that the family will live up to her Norman Rockwell type expectations: home is the site of sustenance and love. But as soon as Shelly enters the home, she realizes that none of her expectations will be fulfilled. Because Shelly is an outsider, though, she is a "nice door for the audience" (Woodruff 155). Through her character, we see the dysfunctional nature of this home. It would appear, then, that Shelly gains status as a spectator, the possessor of the look. As an outsider, she watches, observes, and objectifies the action of the play. However, she is not entirely privileged, for she is part of the play. She does not entirely occupy the masculine position of spectator, for as character, she is herself spectacle. What is important, however, is that Shepard has the audience identify with a female character here, perhaps another strategy that undercuts the power of the men in the play. Shelly sees more clearly than the other characters who are caught up in the operations of a dead system and institution. Ironically, Shelly uses conventional female domestic activities to defend herself from her odd surroundings. When Vince turns to her for the existential reassurance his family cannot provide, Shelly deflects his objectifying desire by telling him: "You're the one who wants to stay. So I'll stay. I'll stay and I'll cut carrots. And I'll cook the carrots. And I'll do whatever I have to do to survive. Just to make it through this" (94). These "feminine" activities provide sustenance to Shelly. However, for Vince they appear trivial. For reassurance, he turns to the family photo album, framed familial objects from the past. Even though he holds the script, it is not enough, so he takes off for the great outdoors in search of his identity that no one in the home will confirm.

With Vince absent, the eccentric behavior of the men intensifies. All of them want Shelly's attention; all of them want Shelly to mirror their desires. Tilden, for example, wants Shelly to remain silent and listen to his story about the dead baby. Dodge wants her to wait on him. And when Bradley tells her to "stay put," he symbolically rapes her by putting his hand in her mouth. The gesture is a disturbing one, but because Bradley uses a prosthetic penis, his hand, his patriarchal power is questioned at the very moment he is trying to prove his potency. Later, his impotence is confirmed. Shelly manipulates and torments him by taking away his artificial leg.

When Halie returns in the third act, she not only finds Shelly in control, but she herself has undergone a miraculous transformation. She is lively and out of mourning. Her change, however, is only superficial. She is still male-identified, and her male companion, Father Dewis, is impotent, too. As he tells her, he cannot accommodate experiences that fall beyond his "parish" (126).

Halie's loyalty to men and to this family is particularly disturbing, given the confession Dodge makes in the third act. We learn that Halie had a baby late in life, when Dodge and she had not been sleeping together. There is even some hint that the baby was born out of a relationship between Halie and Tilden. The hint of the violation of the incest taboo is all important one, since it, according to Lévi-Strauss and Friedrich Engels is the founding principle of patriarchy (Lévi-Strauss 36; Engels 94–146). The fact that women were always sure of their offspring but men were not resulted in rigorous legislation and oppression of female sexuality and the construction of the incest taboo. Whether the incestuous relationship actually occurred is never entirely revealed, but the violation, incestuous or not, is great and symbolic of the threat feminine sexuality poses for patriarchy.

As a mother within the phallic economy, Halie had an obligation to fulfill—to insure the patriarchal lineage and retain its purity. Halie, a mother, must have a man, either a husband or son, in order to exist within the phallic economy. While upholding the prescribed desires for women in patriarchy, Halie has also violated them by taking the patriarchal admonitions too far. She must bear a son, not copulate with one. Therefore, she must be punished. Dodge mentions that he forced Halie to give birth at home in order to make delivery painful. Because the child's conception was so "unnatural," Dodge did not expect the child to live. When it does, Dodge "drowned it. Just like the runt of the litter" (124). Halie may be the keeper of the family tree, but she cannot add new branches without the law of the father.

The decision to kill Halie's child illustrates that anything created outside the father's control is nonexistent. Further, since it was a male child, Dodge has again castrated Halie, depriving her of the usual reward for women in patriarchy. By taking the child away, Dodge forces Halie outside of the phallic economy. This act may explain Halie's obsession with replacement masculine figures. She attaches herself desperately to the cultural trappings of patriarchy—monuments, priests, and her remaining sons—in order to fulfill this double castration, this double lack that Dodge has forced upon her.

—Ann C. Hall, *"A Kind of Alaska"*: *Women in the Plays of O'Neill, Pinter and Shepard*, (Illinois: Southern Illinois University Press, 1993): 97-100.

True West

True West's two central characters, Austin and Lee, have such opposing temperaments that critics often see them as representing two sides of a single self, or a single myth. Austin exemplifies the New West commercialism, social conformity, intellectual elitism, and the rational control of artistic intuition, while Lee stands for the Old West survivalism, rebellious wanderlust, horse sense, and the triumph of the spontaneous tall tale. Both men depend on one another as much as they war with each other; the same may be said of Hollywood glitz and the coyote-like savagery that negotiates it, the rational mind and the intuition that flouts it, and artistic impulsiveness and the technical constraints that dog it. And again one of Shepard's recurring ghosts haunts the characters: the infirm, ineffectual, alcoholic father who subtly and inexorably drives his sons' fragile identities. The autobiographical elements of this play are many: Shepard's own artistic nonconformism and his resistance to the commercialism of Broadway, his move to Northern California once successful, and his own alcoholic father.

Act One, Scene One takes place in the kitchen and adjoining alcove in the Los Angeles home of Austin's and Lee's mother, the setting for all of the action in the play. As the scene opens, Austin sits at a glass table writing by candlelight (crucial to his artistic process) while Lee, drinking beer, prods him with questions. Austin, an ivy-leaguer and successful movie screenwriter, has traveled from his home in Northern California to housesit for his mother and meet his producer Saul about a script. Lee, a desert dweller with a filthy T-shirt and two days' worth of facial hair growth, is visiting for an indefinite period of time and is primarily concerned with using Austin's car.

The following morning (Scene Two) finds Austin watering the plants and Lee drinking a beer. Lee has spent the night walking in the San Gabriel "foothills," peeping his head into the windows of suburban families and admiring their dreamlike existence. Lee tells Austin that he lived on the Mojave desert alone for three months as a result of "passing through" there on his way to see their father.

Austin, quite opposite in character, confesses that he could never be away from people for that long and goes crazy just staying alone in a hotel room. Austin asks Lee to leave before his producer arrives to discuss a movie deal with him—something Lee translates as "hustling"—and finally agrees to lend Lee his car.

Scene Three begins that afternoon as Austin and his producer Saul Kimmer discuss the potential of Austin's script idea to attract a major star and get him a large advance. Suddenly Lee enters carrying a stolen T.V. set. Within minutes Lee interests Saul in playing a game of golf with him, and by the end of the scene, Saul has agreed to consider an idea Lee says he has for a western movie. Austin is commissioned to type out the outline for Lee. When Saul leaves, all Austin can do is demand his car keys back from a smiling Lee.

By Scene Four, night has fallen and Lee is dictating a plot summary of his movie to Austin, who is typing it. Perhaps intentionally, perhaps out of sheer naivete, Lee insists on every detail and expects Austin to know when to edit him and when to retain the integrity of his crude words. Austin, a self-proclaimed true artist, grows exasperated with Lee's painstakingly bad story, calling the plot points too convenient and the events too fake. An argument ensues in which Lee tells Austin "get off your high horse," and threatens to steal his car if he does not continue writing. The argument then subsides as Austin encourages Lee, who has begun to think he'd rather dismantle trucks for a living than write a script. The idea of two diametrically opposed minds trying to collaborate on telling a story is both humorous and far-reaching in its implications. In this one exchange, Shepard manages to merge three conflicts: the desert duel, the divided artistic mind, and adult brothers falling into childish dispute when at the home of their mother.

Scene five begins Act Two and takes place the next morning. Lee has returned from his golf game with Saul and brags to Austin that as a result of losing a bet that Lee could sink a fifty-foot putt, Saul is going to pick up his movie idea—with Austin as the scriptwriter— and drop Austin's script. A shocked and angry Austin demands his car keys from Lee, claiming he needs to go out for a drive and do some thinking. Lee convinces him to stay, pouring both of them a drink of champagne.

That afternoon (Scene Six), Saul has arrived. Austin accuses Saul of falling for Lee's hustling and refuses to write the script. But Saul has become enamored of Lee's old-western style and boasts that three movie studios are fighting for the script. Saul has agreed, at Lee's request, to put some of the advance money in trust for their father, while Austin laments that their father drank away all the money he ever gave him. Here one sees that beneath the apparent struggle between brothers for artistic recognition is the familiar competition for the father's love—in this case an abandoning father whose love can never be bought.

In Scene Seven, a role reversal between the two brothers has taken place: it is now Lee who is typing a script by candlelight and Austin who is idly drinking. This technique of reversal, which lends a surreal or transformational quality to the characters' textures, is a common one in Shepard's work. It may point to the opaqueness of identity itself, or perhaps the sense that Austin and Lee are really two sides of the same coin. Yet Lee cannot type and Austin cannot handle his liquor. Austin gets the idea to steal just like Lee, and Lee bets that Austin could not even stomach stealing a toaster. Austin agrees to help Lee type the script if Lee promises to disappear afterwards. This leads Austin into telling a story about their alcoholic father, who hitchhiked to Mexico with a bleeding mouth to get his teeth pulled and dentures made for cheap. Soon after, when out at a bar with Austin, he put his teeth in a bag with the leftover Chop Suey from dinner, and left the bag at the bar. Here Shepard has created a picture that is both hilarious and tragic: this is the father whose love the two brothers have competed for all their lives.

As Scene Eight opens between night and dawn the next day, Lee is alternately smashing the typewriter with a golf club and throwing pages of his script into a burning bowl on the floor of the alcove. Austin is shining up his many stolen toasters, which are all lined up on the counter next to the TV. Empty whiskey bottles and beer cans lie on the floor and the two drunk men share a half-empty bottle. When Austin begins to romanticize the desert and imagines dropping everything and living there, Lee is insulted because his life in the desert is one of necessity, not choice. He violently knocks a plate out of Austin's hand, sending toast flying and then crushing it with his feet. Then he and Austin make a deal that if Austin writes the script, giving Lee all the credit and all the money, Lee will allow Austin to accompany him to the desert. At this point Austin's conformity has been melted away by the alcohol, and Lee's dreams of a six-figure advance have suddenly made him a stickler for following through.

Scene Nine takes place midday. The stage is "like a desert junkyard at high noon." Austin is seated at the table furiously writing while Lee circles the table dictating and revising. They are surrounded by the debris from their revelry—bottles, a smashed typewriter, a broken phone, and other trash. As they collaborate on the wording of a line, an artistic compatibility arises that seems satisfying to both of them. They are so engrossed that they do not notice the entrance of their mother, who has returned from her trip early. As they tell her about Lee's script deal and their plans to move to the desert together, she remains blandly detached. While Austin clings to the plan that he has made with Lee, Lee begins to doubt it and prepares to leave, which causes a scuffle between the two that results in Austin putting Lee in a chokehold with the telephone cord. Mother remains numb. After struggling mightily, Lee eventually appears to be dead, but as soon as Austin makes a move to leave, Lee jumps up and blocks the door. The lights fade on the two brothers facing each other as a coyote barks in the distance.

True West

Austin is a screenwriter who has come to Los Angeles to housesit for his mother and pitch an idea to his producer, Saul Kimmer. He believes his writing is a true art form, borne of the unique inspiration he receives from being surrounded by the average moviegoer—in traffic, in the Safeway, and other trappings of the new West. When his brother Lee, a beer-swilling, thieving ruffian who has spent several months virtually alone in the desert, stops by and effectively edges Austin out of the limelight with some streetwise hustling and an implausible movie idea, Austin is aghast. He eventually turns to swilling and thieving himself, filling the role of his now suddenly successful brother. His attitude toward Lee alternates between contempt and jealousy; mixed with liquor, they lead him nearly to strangle Lee to death.

Lee is Austin's older brother, and his exact opposite. Where Austin is clean, controlled, Ivy League educated, and spends his time dreaming up stories, Lee is filthy, hedonistic, street-educated, and pursues success with theft and well-calculated wagers. Even though Lee seems barely able to keep clothes on his back, he ironically excels at golf, the millionaire's sport. His fast talking gets him a golf date with Saul, Austin's producer, and his ability to sink a fifty-foot putt lands him a movie deal. Even more ironically, his unseasoned and even childish art of storytelling makes him the talk of the big movie studios within days of meeting Saul. As much as Lee finds Austin's slick snobbery contemptible, he is jealous of his brother and hurt that Austin glibly romanticizes his desert existence. Both men have suffered from a lack of parental care, and when Austin almost chokes Lee to death, a bit of easy trickery on Lee's part gets him out of danger and proves him the superior survivalist.

Saul Kimmer is a slick Hollywood producer who arrives at the house to discuss a deal with Austin for his television script. Though he appears to be an expert manipulator when it comes to getting money from the movie studios, he is easily hustled by Lee onto the golf course, where he finds himself the loser of a high stakes bet. As is common in many of Shepard's plays, Saul functions as the character outside the family who becomes unwittingly embroiled in the family's power struggles—he is the pawn that Lee uses to prove that his ivy league-educated brother is no better than him. His sudden withdrawal of his loyalty from Austin in favor of Lee also serves an important dramatic purpose for Shepard; it brings to the surface a tragically funny competition between the two brothers for the affections of an alcoholic father who does not even acknowledge them.

Mom is Austin's and Lee's mother. She does not appear until the end of the play, when she returns from her trip out of town to find her house, which she left in the care of Austin, in utter shambles. Her demeanor is eerily calm and numb, suggesting a full retreat from the pain of being part of such a family. Somewhat deranged, she interprets a museum advertisement describing the arrival of a Picasso collection as an invitation to meet the artist himself; and ironically, this shows her fit to be the mother of the two brothers whose absurd dreams of glory, either in movies or in desert solitude, lead them to a near-death struggle before her unmoved eyes.

CRITICAL VIEWS ON

True West

[Frank Rich is an op-ed columnist for *The New York Times* and has also served as the paper's chief drama critic. He has written about culture and politics for many publications, including *Time, Esquire,* and *The New Republic.* In this excerpt, Rich argues that despite the lack of good direction at the Public Theater, Shepard's writing successfully envisions the loss of American myths.]

Some day, when the warring parties get around to writing their memoirs, we may actually discover who killed "True West," the Sam Shepard play that finally opened at the Public Theater last night. As the press has already reported, this failure is an orphan. Robert Woodruff, the nominal director, left the play in previews and disowned the production. Mr. Shepard has also disowned the production, although he has not ventured from California to see it. The producer, Joseph Papp, meanwhile, has been left holding the bag. New Year's will be here shortly, and one can only hope that these talented men will forgive and forget.

At least their battle has been fought for a worthwhile cause. "True West" seems to be a very good Shepard play—which means that it's one of the American theater's most precious natural resources. But no play can hold the stage all by itself. Except for odd moments, when Mr. Shepard's fantastic language rips through the theater on its own sinuous strength, the "True West" at the Public amounts to little more than a stand-up run-through of a text that remains to be explored. This play hasn't been misdirected; it really looks as if it hasn't been directed at all.

You know a play has no director when funny dialogue dies before it reaches the audience. Or when two lead actors step on each other's lines and do "business" rather than create characters. Or when entrances and scene-endings look arbitrary rather than preplanned.

Or when big farcical sequences—an avalanche of Coors beer cans, for instance—clatter about the stage creating confusion rather than mirth. Or when an evening's climax—the mystical death embrace of two fratricidal brothers—is so vaguely choreographed it looks like a polka. All these things and more happen, at the Public.

It's a terrible shame. "True West" is a worthy direct descendant of Mr. Shepard's "Curse of the Starving Class" and "Buried Child." Many of his persistent recent themes are present and accounted for—the spiritual death of the American family, the corruption of the artist by business, the vanishing of the Western wilderness and its promised dream of freedom. If the playwright dramatizes his concerns in fantastic flights of poetic imagery, that imagery always springs directly from the life of the people and drama he has invented. Mr. Shepard doesn't graft symbols onto his plays. He's a true artist; his best works are organic creations that cannot be broken down into their constituent parts.

The brothers of "True West" are both hustlers, or, if you win, modern-day cowboys who have lost their range. Lee (Peter Boyle) is a drifter and petty burglar, and the younger Austin (Tommy Lee Jones) is a screenwriter. The play is about what happens when the two men reunite in their mother's ticky-tacky suburban Los Angles home. By the end of the evening, they have stolen each other's identities and destroyed the house, and yet they can never completely sever the ties that bind. Like the heroes in the "true life" Hollywood movie western they write during the course of the play, Lee and Austin are "two lamebrains" doomed to chase each other eternally across a desolate ever-receding frontier.

Mr. Shepard is an awesome writer. When Lee and Austin lament the passing of the West they loved (and that maybe never existed), they launch into respectively loopy, nostalgic monologues about the film "Lonely Are the Brave" and the now-extinct neighborhood of their youth. Amusing as they are; these comic riffs are also moving because they give such full life to Mr. Shepard's conflict between America's myths and the bitter, plastic reality that actually exists. Lee can no longer distinguish the true West from the copy he finds in a movie: Austin discovers that his childhood memories are inseparable from the vistas he sees on cheap post cards. Looking for roots, Mr. Shepard's characters fall into a void.

The playwright also provides motifs involving dogs, crickets, desert topography, cars, household appliances (especially toasters and television sets) and the brothers' unseen, destitute father. As the play progresses, these images keep folding into one another until we are completely transported into the vibrant landscape of Mr. Shepard's imagination. Such is the collective power of this playwright's words that even his wilder conceits seem naturalistic in the context of his play. We never question that Lee would try to destroy a typewriter with a golf club or that the family patriarch would lose his false teeth in a doggie bag full of chop suey.

"True West" slips only when Mr. Shepard, a master of ellipses, tries to fill in the blanks. Does he really need lines like, "There's nothing real here now, least of all me," or, "There's no such thing as the West anymore"? The movie-industry gags, most of which involve a producer in gold chains (Louis Zorich), are jarring as well. Mr. Shepard's witticisms about development deals and agents have been written funnier by Woody Allen, and Paul Mazursky, and they bring "True West" down to earth.

—Frank Rich, "Myth vs. Reality," *New York Times*, 24 December 1980. *The New York Times Theater Reviews* (1979-80): 456.

WILLIAM KLEB ON OLD WEST AND NEW WEST AS MEANINGLESS MIRAGES

[Willam Kleb has been a contributing editor of *Theater* and has been published in *Performing Arts Journal*. In this excerpt, Kleb argues that Shepard depicts the old west, through Lee, as an empty dream, and the new west, through Austin, as a mirage.]

A second theme in *True West* raises similar questions. It has to do with the nature of the American West. As his title implies, Shepard is asking what is the true, or real, West. Again the two brothers dramatize the metaphor, but, in a sense, they are simply stand-ins for Mom and the Old Man. The Old Man (and Lee) are clearly remnants of what Gary Snyder in *The Old Ways* calls the "first phase" of western "exploitation"—an "epic" or "heroic" period, at least in retrospect, characterized by images of manliness, vigor, mobility, unpredictability, rootlessness, humor and violence. It is a world that stands in direct opposition to the world of Mom (and Austin). These two represent the "new west"—the West of suburbs and freeways; toasters and color TVs; Cocker Spaniels and house plants; Safeway. Shepard's treatment of Mom and her world is harsh: he trashes her kitchen and kills her plants; his portrait of her is satiric. She may seem less vividly "the Terrible Mother" than Halie in *Buried Child*, but her weird, iconographic presence seems just as threatening and life-denying. Moreover, like Ella, the mother in *The Curse of the Starving Class*, Mom is infected with what Shepard considers the most serious new-western sickness—alienation from the land. No wonder she seems flat, remote, lifeless, unreal. In fact, although at first this non-western landscape appears to be the most real world in True West—after all, the kitchen, its major symbol, is really there, in three dimensions on the stage—it becomes, ironically, a fantasy, a kind of mirage. Austin's metamorphosis makes him aware of this truth and increases his desperation to get to the desert. Initially, he insists that his world (and Mom's) is the only real or true one, and that he, not Lee, is really "in touch" with it: "I drive on the freeway every day! I swallow the smog! I watch the news in color! I shop in the Safeway!" But after this humiliation and transformation, he doesn't "recognize the place" anymore; it reminds him of the "'50s"; it lacks substance and has nothing for him now. A few moments later, Mom echoes Austin's words almost exactly: "I can't stay here," she says, wandering vaguely out of her kitchen. "This is worse than being homeless ... I don't recognize this place."

On the other hand, Shepard's attitude toward the Old West does not seem, in the final analysis, much more favorable. Lee, its representative, may be the most vital and amusing character in *True West*, but he is also violent and devious, childish and totally self-absorbed; actually he envies Austin and even admits that he lives as he does only because he can't "make it" in Austin's world. And the Old Man seems, ultimately, nothing more than an eccentric drunk. Gary Snyder remarks that the "first phase" West was "in a sense psychologically occupied by boys without fathers and mothers, who are really free to get away with things for a while..." In fact, Lee and the Old Man are not adults, fathers, they are old boys (males to be sure). Creation is a kind of play and the artist (as Picasso demonstrated) must remain, in part at least, a child; if a sandbox is necessary to sustain the illusion, then into the sandbox. But in *True West*, Shepard's sandbox, the desert, seems just as immaterial, or unreal, as Mom's suburbs or Lee himself; the Old Man, after all, doesn't even appear on stage—he is a rumor, a ghost, a memory. In *Angel City*, Shepard uses film as a metaphor for the uneasy relationship between illusion and reality (surely an analogy that should be retired by now), and Lee's film script, predictably, makes Shepard's point about the Old West explicit. Lee insists that his is a "true story," yet it seems, in the telling, just another tall tale; it may have what Kimmer calls "the ring of truth" (i.e., archetypic resonance), but it also seems just as fake and contrived as Austin maintains. If it does say "something about the land," that land—that mythic western landscape—is becoming more and more remote, "a dead issue," as Austin puts it before his re-birth. In short, in *True West*, past and present both dissolve; Lee and Austin are left frozen, "stuck" between an empty dream and an insubstantial reality.

—William Kleb, "Worse than Being Homeless: True West and the Divided Self," *American Dreams: The Imagination of Sam Shepard*, ed. Bonnie Marranca (New York: Performing Arts Journal Publications, 1981): 122-123.

TUCKER ORBISON ON THE PLAY'S DRAMATIZATION OF THE SELF AND THE SECOND SELF

[Tucker Orbison is the author of *The Tragic Vision of John Ford* (1974) and the coeditor of *The Binding of Proteus: Perspectives on Myth and the Literary Process* (1980). In this excerpt, Orbison applies C.F. Keppler's theory of the split psychic entity to the characters of Austin and Lee.]

In a recent interview with Susan Sontag, the editors of *Performing Arts Journal* made the statement, "Consciousness is the principal subject of modern art," and Shepard, in the same issue, expressed his agreement: "The only thing which still remains [from the sixties] and still persists as the single most important idea is the idea of consciousness."[14] He specified more precisely what he meant when, in a letter to Patrick Fennell, he explained, "I'm interested in states of mind, in mystery, in psychotic behavior, in possession, in trance states, in magic."[15] Shepard would agree with D.H. Lawrence that "the inscrutable well-heads whence the living self bubbles up ... must ever remain a mystery."[16] Still, *True West* does shed some light on this mystery. One may speculate, for example, that just as Natty Bumppo in *The Pioneers* could be seen by Lawrence as Cooper's true inner self, Austin and Lee are alternate selves of Shepard.[17] A more useful approach for our purposes, perhaps, will be to notice that Shepard's characters "appear out of nowhere" in such a way as to bear a close psychic resemblance to each other. It can be argued, in fact, that Lee and Austin together form dual, opposed elements in a single self.

The first impressions of Lee and Austin, as made for example in New York's Cherry Lane production in 1982–1984,[18] create a sense of such dissimilarity that the two hardly seem brothers at all. Thus, Austin is neat and clean, Lee messy and dirty; Austin's hair is combed, Lee's is tousled; Austin wears a white shirt with collar, Lee an old T-shirt; Austin is cleanshaven, Lee has a day's growth of beard. Austin's speech is proper, clear, and restrained; Lee's is foul, drunkenly slurred, and from time to time furiously uncontrolled. All the more puzzling for an audience, then, when Shepard gradually reveals that they are in some ways identical. Indeed, at the beginning of scene 7 the two switch roles.

This *coup de théâtre* is, however, carefully prepared for. When, in scene 4, Austin agrees to help Lee write a screenplay, Lee becomes sarcastic: "I'll just turn myself right inside out. I could be just like you then, huh? Sittin' around dreamin' stuff up. Gettin' paid to dream" (p. 25). Before the scene ends, both brothers explain how they used to daydream about what it would be like to be the other:

> LEE. I always wondered what'd be like to be you.
>> AUSTIN You did?
> LEE. Yeah, sure. I used to picture you walkin' around some campus
>> with yer arms fulla' books. Blondes chasin' after ya'.
> AUSTIN. Blondes? That's funny.
> LEE. What's funny about it?
> AUSTIN. Because I always used to picture you somewhere.... And I

> used to say to myself, "Lee's got the right idea. He's out
> there in the world and here I am. What am I doing?" (p. 26)

Two different impressions are made here. Shepard introduces the idea of internal similarity under the external differences and reveals the yearning of each to be like the other. Lee and Austin are psychically related, it appears, in the same way C.F. Keppler describes the relation between a self and a second self:

> But what then *is* the second self? The answer is given us by what has just been said about the two main spurious second selves that are so often taken for it: the fact that what each of them lacks is exactly what the other possesses. The objective second self possesses external reality, clearly independent of the first self.... The subjective second self does share a basic psychical identity with the first self.... It is [the] quality of paradox that makes the second self so difficult a figure to talk about.... He is always "there," a self in his own right, never translatable into a product of mental aberration; yet he is always "here" as well, his psyche intergrown by untraceable shared tendrils with that of his counterpart....[19]

In short, the second self is subjectively identified with the first and at the same time is objectively an opposite.

Is it Austin, or is it Lee, who is the second self? Keppler points out that "the second self always suggests some aspect of the first self that has been suppressed or unrealized", he always "intrude[s] into the life of the first", and he is "responsible for the dynamic tension that always exists between them. He is the self that has been left behind, or overlooked, or unrealized, or otherwise excluded from the first self's self-conception; he is the self that must be come to terms with".[20] Clearly, then, Lee is Austin's second self, Austin the first self or ego. Separately, they form the archetypal pattern of the hostile brothers, the elder violent and often unrestrained, the younger self-possessed and controlled. Together, they comprise opposite sides of one psychic entity.

NOTES

[14] "on Art and Consciousness," *Performing Arts Journal*, 2 (Fall 1977), 29; Special Section [Sam Shepard et al.], "American Experimental Theatre: Then and Now," *Performing Arts Journal*, 2 (Fall 1977), 14.

15 Patrick J. Fennell, "Sam Shepard: The Flesh and Blood of Theatre," Unpubl. diss., Univ. of California, Santa Barbara, 1977, p. 18.

16 D.H. Lawrence, *The Symbolic Meaning: The uncollected versions of "Studies in Classic American Literature,"* ed. Armin Arnold (London, 1962), p. 74. Shepard has, in fact, written: "A character for me is a composite of different mysteries. He's an unknown quantity" ("Language, Visualization and the Inner Library," p. 217).

17 William Kleb, "Worse Than Being Homeless: *True West* and the Divided Self," in *American Dreams*, p. 124, has developed this idea in some detail.

18 The Cherry Lane production was *True West*'s second New York run. As is widely known, the play's first New York run was unsuccessful, largely because Joseph Papp's interference caused   Robert Woodruff, who had directed the successful première in San Francisco, to resign. As a result, Shepard himself disowned the production.

19 C.F. Keppler, *The Literature of the Second Self* (Tucson, Ariz., 1972), pp. 9–10.

20 Ibid., pp. 9, 11.

—Tucker Orbison, "Mythic Levels in Shepard's True West." *Modern Drama* 27, no. 4 (December 1984): 512-514.

DAVID J. DEROSE ON THE SUPRAREAL STAGING IN THE PLAY

[David J. DeRose's essays on Sam Shepard have appeared in *Theater, American Theatre,* and *Theatre Journal*. In this excerpt, DeRose argues that the toaster scene exemplifies Shepard's art of "suprareal" staging: imposing realistic effects on surreal events.]

Perhaps the most memorable stage image in *True West* is the opening of scene 8, the "typewriter-toasters" scene, in which Shepard offers a tour de force of suprareal staging. At the end of the previous scene, Lee was left pounding out a script on the typewriter as Austin stumbled off into the night, determined to prove himself to his brother by stealing a toaster. Scene 8 opens several hours later:

Very early morning, between night and day. No crickets, coyotes yapping feverishly in distance before light comes up, a small fire blazes up in the dark from alcove area, sound of LEE smashing typewriter with a golf club, lights coming up, LEE seen smashing typewriter methodically then dropping pages of his script into a burning bowl set on the floor of alcove, flames leap up, AUSTIN has a whole bunch of stolen toasters lined up on the sink counter along with LEE's stolen TV, the toasters are of a wide variety of models, mostly chrome, AUSTIN goes up and down the line of toasters, breathing on them and polishing them with a dish towel, both men are drunk, empty whiskey bottles and beer cans litter the floor of kitchen.... LEE keeps periodically taking deliberate ax-chops at the typewriter, using a nine-iron[.] (*TW*, 42–43)

In this scene, the psychologically farfetched transformation of the two brothers is provided with both a material grounding and a sharp surreal edge by the introduction of suprareal staging techniques. Shepard's disruption of ordered reality is physically anchored in the use of several operative toasters popping up burnt toast throughout the scene and a previously functional typewriter rendered into a lump of twisted metal by the persistent swing of Lee's nine iron. The toast is carefully buttered, only to be scattered across the floor, the contents of the kitchen drawers and cabinets are strewn across the stage, and the phone is literally ripped from the wall. This wonderful Walpurgisnacht of suprarealism is so accurate in its reproduction of material reality that one loses track of where the rational action ends and the surreal takes over. As William Kleb noted in his review of the original Magic Theatre production, "objective and subjective realities are not juxtaposed [as they were in many of Shepard's earlier plays], they are superimposed."[17]

Once Shepard draws the audience into the undomesticated midnight landscape of the second act, like the unseen coyotes in the play who lure "innocent pets away from their homes," he sheds the light of day on his creation. In the midday heat of the final scene, "all the debris from the previous scene is now starkly visible in intense yellow light" (*TW*, 50); Mom's clean, tidy kitchen has been transformed into a "desert junkyard." To accentuate the distance he has taken his audience, Shepard suddenly redirects the flow of the action by introducing a new character whose unintegrated presence, like the thugs at the end of *Curse of the Starving Class*, is completely foreign to the stage environment. The surreal intruder is none other than Mom herself, who has returned from the Alaskan frontier. While her presence might not have seemed unreal at the play's beginning, by the end of the play the stage has been transformed into a wasteland in which Mom, an anemic and emotionless little woman, dressed in white with matching red shoes, shoulder bag, and luggage, is completely out of place. She has cut short her vacation to the Alaskan wilds in order to return to the civility of her home. Upon entering, however, she is confronted by a savage battle between her sons that leaves her feeling "worse than being homeless." Her reaction, however, is completely bland, completely disproportionate to the wreckage in her kitchen and the violent struggle of her two sons. "You boys shouldn't fight in the house," she drones, as Lee and Austin pose on the verge of killing each other.

In the light of day and with his mother's entrance, Lee quickly dismisses the previous night's dreamlike activities, abandoning the script and his aspirations as a scriptwriter. Austin, however, is not as willing to drop his newly adopted persona. When Lee decides to back out of an earlier promise to take Austin to the desert, Austin turns savage. Throwing Lee to the floor and wrapping the phone cord around his neck, he chokes Lee until the older brother falls limp in his arms.

In the final moments of the play, Shepard creates an archetypal image that both encompasses and transcends all that has preceded it. With Lee lying motionless on the floor, Austin is free to take the car and escape into the desert. In the first act, he told Lee, "We're not insane. We're not driven to acts of violence" (*TW*, 24). But in this final scene, as if to prove the complete adoption of his new primal persona, Austin expresses the remorselessness of his newly uncovered violence. With the phone cord still wrapped around his brother's neck, he tells his mother: "I can kill him! I can easily kill him. Right now. Right here" (*TW*, 58). At the moment of his escape, however, Austin hesitates. Moral consciousness seems to creep back into his psyche as he stares at the inert body of his brother. In that instant of hesitation, Lee is on his feet, blocking Austin's escape. The lights suddenly change as the two brothers "square off to each other ... the figures of the brothers now appear to be caught in a vast desert-like landscape, they are very still but watchful for the next move, lights go slowly to black as the after-image of the brothers pulses in the dark, coyote fades" (*TW*, 59). This final image is not a resolution, as Shepard himself has pointed out, but a timeless confrontation. The pulsing of the after-image suspends the moment in time and space, transporting it beyond the relatively realistic realm of the play. It is a "postplay" (in the sense of "posthypnotic") suggestion in which the brothers are transformed into archetypal figures, facing off, fighting hopelessly on against the backdrop of eternity. In Austin's moment of hesitation arises the germ of moral consciousness that forever separates him from Lee and places him at irresolvable odds with the amoral "Lee" in himself. As Ross Wetzsteon said of his moving exposure to the final image of Shepard's *La Turista*, it was a moment that "dramatized the themes of the play far more precisely than could any words, an image that communicated the emotional texture of the characters' lives far more vividly than could any speech" (Wetzsteon 1984, 1–2).

NOTE

17 William, Kleb, "Worse Than Being Homeless: *True West* and the Divided Self," *American Dreams*, ed. Bonnie Marranca (New York: Performing Arts Journal Publications, 1981), 121.

—David J. DeRose, *Sam Shepard*, (New York: Twayne Publishers, 1992): 111-113.

MARTIN TUCKER ON THE PLAY'S COMEDIC LIGHTNESS

[Martin Tucker is the editor of *Literary Exile in the Twentieth Century: An Analysis and Biographical Dictionary* (1991). In this excerpt, Tucker calls the play Shepard's "least troubled" work and explores the ways in which the play's theme of foolish passion is ultimately reassuring.]

True West, the third in Shepard's family plays, is on the surface Shepard's most realistic play, but the surface is only part of the story. The realistic setting, and the seeming realistic description and linear narrative unfolding, is emphasized by Shepard in his stage directions, where Shepard explicitly writes that no distortions in the shape of real objects or colors should be made in the setting, and no distractions should compete for the focus of the play, which is the "evolution of the characters' situation."

True West was first produced at the Magic Theatre in San Francisco in July 1980 under the direction of Robert Woodruff. It was brought to New York for Joseph Papp's New York Shakespeare Festival/Public Theater and opened there on December 23, 1980.

Papp replaced Woodruff as the director after the two differed on the presentation. Shepard denounced the Papp decision to replace Woodruff but allowed the production to continue; Shepard was out of town on movie work at the time.

If Shepard chooses realism and a more conventional linear narrative as his style and mode in this play, the story beneath the observed circumstances and character has a familiar continuity in its rhetorical questioning of social responsibility and artistic endeavor. Other familiar elements are apparent in the work: the coyote, and its contrasting complement of desert life, the cricket, sound their note of attention. The two brothers, Lee and Austin, are in a sense the human parallels of the coyote and the cricket: Lee is the loner and desert rat proclaiming his fruitless independence in the dark desert air; Austin is the conscientious writer clacking/chirping away at his typewriter in his production of stories. Austin is too self-conscious to call his work "art," though such a declaration would be no more self-conscious than his denial of artistic desire and enterprise. What Austin lacks is the self-conscious commitment—the arrogance of his own worth and distinction—of the true artist. His brother Lee, on the other hand, possesses the arrogance of the artist but none of the discipline, or the desire for such discipline. Lee lacks the humility of the artist, as necessary a component of the true artist as an acceptance of the special distinction that sets artists apart from their fellow human beings.

While seemingly different, the brothers are complementary aspects of the artist. When the movie producer Saul Kimmer says he believes the two brothers are one, the ideal of the two selves of the artist is made explicit. But, as Shepard shows, the selves do not cohere—they are always at war. Lee recognizes this inalterable fact when he tells his brother that most murders are committed in the family, and most family murders are those committed by brother against brother. (...)

In *True West* the father does not appear physically but his presence is felt. The two brothers refer to the father several times, and they are rivals for his approval/affection. They do not verbalize their trips to the desert to see the father as a journey of homage, but their behavior and their imagery tell the truth. Each wants the father's blessing wholly. The father gives neither his blessing, because he is not capable of passing on a power that is only illusion. His patrimony exists in the mind, but in this case the legacy is more delusion than inspiration. In the desert the father is a bedouin king; to acknowledge his sons with a resolution of approval would be to introduce the same fears and tremblings the father experienced in the world outside his desert shelter. One of the memory-accented references in the play concerns the contact each of the brothers makes with the father. Austin has given him money, and is angry because the father spent it on liquor. Lee has given his father the compliment of imitation—Lee understands the father's spurning of Austin's bourgeois-conditioned allegiances.

The father becomes the apex of the triad of the West, with the two sons, or two sides of the son, at each angle of the triangle. The play does not resolve the question of the true West—Los Angeles or Needles, California, urban house or Mojave Desert trailer, social conformity or independent drifting—but it presents the conflict in one of Shepard's most haunting, and frightening, images. As the play ends, the two brothers are alone on stage, at each other's throats, each blocking the other's way out of the room, each poised to kill the other. The question that arises and remains long after the brilliantly frightening image is the one of wonder whether Shepard is presenting a mythic drama in which one brother must kill another in order to survive, in which the artist, in all his guises, and the responsible citizen, in all his working shifts, must continue to war with each other. Though Bertolt Brecht's influence on Shepard was long ago absorbed into Shepard's unique view of things, the ending of *True West* has a Brechtian air of epic alienation.

—Martin Tucker, *Sam Shepard*, (New York: The Continuum Publishing Company, 1992): 136-7, 138-140

HENRY I. SCHVEY ON THE PLAY AS REFLECTION OF SHEPARD'S ATTITUDES TOWARD HIS FATHER

[Henry I. Schvey is the author of *Oskar Kokoschka: The Painter as Playwright* (1982). In this excerpt, Schvey traces the play's contradictory portrayal of father-son relationship back to Shepard's own life.]

The thread which connects the various phases of Shepard's work, despite their obvious disparity, is the image of the father. Occasionally a figure of strength, virility, or rude wisdom, he is also frequently portrayed as distant, weak, and manipulative. (...)

Shepard's father was a pilot in the Army Air Corps in Italy, having joined the army after his grandfather lost the family farm during the Depression. Returning from combat wounded and apparently emotionally disturbed, Shepard's father became an alcoholic who left the family on numerous occasions for a solitary life in the desert. Despite his son's increasing popularity and fame, his father remained an enigmatic and reclusive figure living in the desert surrounded by his Second World War flying mementoes, who spent the food money his son gave him on bourbon. He died in 1983 after being hit by a car near his home in Santa Fe. He only saw one of Shepard's plays during his lifetime, *Buried Child*, and on that occasion was so drunk that he stood up during the production and began talking to the characters on stage.

In addition to his alcoholism and reclusiveness, Shepard's father was a man of colorful stories and poetry. He attended college on the G.I. Bill, taught high school geography and Spanish, and even studied at the University of Bogota on a Fulbright scholarship. Shepard has called his father "a poet himself in a certain way ... in a certain weird way. Because of circumstances he never really had the chance to prove himself. Who knows if my work is better than his? That has nothing to do with it. One thing that I'll always be eternally grateful to him for was that he introduced me to García Lorca when I was a kid—in Spanish, no less ... He told me all about García Lorca's life with the gypsies and all that."[13]

However, despite the elder Rogers's influence on his son poetically, it is clear that their relationship was also filled with conflict and the feeling of perpetual abandonment even before the father left the house for good. "It was always hit and miss, always hit and miss," Shepard's sister Roxanne has said. "There was always a kind of facing off between them and it was Sam who got the bad end of that. Dad was a tricky character. Because he was a charismatic guy when he wanted to be—warm, loving, kind of a hoot to be around. And the other side was a snapping turtle. With him and Sam it was that male thing. You put two virile men in a room and they're going to test each other."[14]

The conflict between son and father remained unresolved even after the latter's death. When asked if his feelings toward his father had changed after his father's fatal accident, Shepard commented: "My relationship with him is the same. Exactly the same. It's a relationship of absolute unknowing. I never knew him, although he was around all the time. There's no point in dwelling on it. I mean, my relationship with him now is exactly the same as when he was alive. It's just as mysterious."[15]

Unravelling the mystery behind his absent father has been a lifelong preoccupation of Shepard's, and the driving force behind many of his most successful plays. Surely it is revealing that Shepard tells us that his father "was around all the time," since this is factually untrue. However, it is true that he was around all the time in Shepard's inner world, even when the young man tried to cast him off. Shortly after arriving on New York's Lower East Side in 1963, bussing tables at the Village Gate and exploring the burgeoning off-off Broadway theater scene that resulted in the Café La Mama, Caffe Cino, and Theater Genesis, Sam Shepard chose to change his name from Steve Rogers to Sam Shepard: "My name, Samuel Shepard Rogers, was too long, ... so I just dropped the *Rogers* part of it. It had been in the family for seven generations and my grandmother wasn't too happy over it."[16] In deliberate imitation of Sam Sheperd, the midwestern doctor who murdered his wife in the early sixties, Steve Rogers chose to "murder" his father by cutting himself off from seven generations of Rogers males. (...)

In *True West*, Shepard transforms his conflicted sensibility toward his father into the opposition between two brothers, Austin and Lee. Austin, the successful Hollywood screenwriter, clearly represents the side of Shepard that has accommodated itself to material success, the aspects that have moved him from his counter-culture roots in the off-off Broadway theater movement of the sixties to a commercially successful career as a film star. Lee, although presented as Austin's brother in the play, is in fact his alter-ego, the part of Shepard's divided self that is rough and crude, lives outside the law, and is drawn toward the elusive image of his father. The play, then, is not so much a bout between two brothers as it is an externalized metaphor of the dialectic between the dual aspects of Shepard's psyche. Although the play is set in their mother's home in a Southern California suburb complete with green synthetic grass floor, the yapping sounds of the coyote of Southern California are continually present in the background, especially in Scenes Seven and Eight, and in Scene Nine when the visual effect is described as being *"like a desert junkyard at high noon, the coolness of the preceding scenes is totally obliterated."*[23] Thus the conflict fought out between the brothers is also projected into the stage setting. (...)

In the play's final tableau, Shepard creates a miraculous image of the "connectedness" between these opposed aspects of a single self. Austin, finding the physically more powerful Lee about to go back to the desert from whence he came, strangles him with a telephone cord to make him stay. The play ironically ends with their mother's departure, as the two sons square off in a *"vast desert-like landscape"* (60). Trapped by the umbilical cord of their connectedness, neither brother can escape, and they are doomed to continue their struggle indefinitely.

NOTES

[13] Cited in Kevin Sessums, "Sam Shepard: Geography of a Horse Dreamer," in *Interview*, 18:9 (September, 1988), 76.

[14] Cited in Samuel G. Freedman, "Sam Shepard's Portrait of the American Family," *International Herald Tribune*, 6 December 1985: 7.

[15] Sessums, 75.

[16] Oumano, 22.

[23] Sam Shepard, *True West*, in *Sam Shepard: Seven Plays*, 50. Subsequent page references are to this edition and will appear in the text.

—Henry I. Schvey, "A Worm in the Wood: The Father-Son Relationship in the Plays of Sam Shepard." *Modern Drama* 36, 1 (March 1993): 13, 14-15, 19, 20, 21.

JEFFREY D. HOEPER ON AUSTIN AND LEE AS CAIN AND ABEL

[Jeffrey D. Hoeper is the coauthor and coeditor of a number of college textbooks, including *Concise Companion to Literature* (1980), *Purpose and Process* (1989), and *Poetry* (1990). In this excerpt, Hoeper traces the correspondences between the sibling rivalry in the play and the biblical story of Cain and Abel.]

The play's plot harks back to the archetypal story of Cain and Abel—in the Byronic variant in which Cain, the peaceful tiller of the soil, is a sympathetic figure, while Abel, the smug slaughterer of sheep, is inexplicably favored by a bloodthirsty deity. As in Genesis, the action takes place to the east of Eden. Shepard sets his play *"in a Southern California suburb, about 40 miles east of Los Angeles."*[3] Lee describes the suburban homes as being "Like a paradise" (12) and Austin subsequently comments, "This is a Paradise down here.... We're livin' in a Paradise" (39).

Granted, these references to Paradise have the informality of a cliché and the sibling rivalry between Austin and Lee is a fairly hackneyed literary motif; nevertheless, the biblical story of Cain is part of our common cultural heritage, and any story of fraternal battle recalls it in some measure. Further, the more closely one looks at Shepard's play, the more reminders there are of the pre-Christian conflict between Cain and Abel. (...)

At the beginning of *True West* there are hints of this pre-Christian conflict between the patriarchal and matriarchal orders. The play is set in the mother's home. Her neighborhood is like Paradise. Her home is filled with vegetation:

> *The windows look out to bushes and citrus trees. The alcove is filled with all sorts of house plants in various spots, mostly Boston ferns hanging in planters at different levels. The floor of the alcove is composed of green synthetic grass.* (3)

Her plants are being served by a dutiful son. Her name is given as "mother" or "Mom," nothing more.

In coming down from the lush north to write a romantic screenplay, Austin may be said to be acting in the service of love (or Aphrodite) and his earnings will be used to support his wife and children. His decision to write by candlelight reflects his attempt to establish a romantic mood appropriate to the story he is striving to create. Like Cain, Austin is associated with vegetation; in his mother's absence, he has vowed to tend her nourishing house plants. The first lines in Scene 1 underscore that duty, and Scene 2 opens with Austin *"watering plants with a vaporizer"* (10). Like Abel, however, Austin is the younger of two brothers and he is clearly the better brother—kind, industrious, and moral.

In contrast, Lee comes up from the desert, like the nomadic Hebrews at the end of their exodus and the beginning of their conquest of Canaan. Somewhere in that vast desert Lee has communed with the "old man"—the father, whom Austin in his prosperity has apparently abandoned. Lee is Austin's sinister opposite, and his questionable character is clearly suggested by his appearance:

> *filthy white t-shirt, tattered brown overcoat covered with dust, dark blue baggy suit pants from the Salvation Army, pink suede belt, pointed black forties dress shoes scuffed up, holes in the soles, no socks, no hat, long pronounced side-burns, "Gene Vincent" hairdo, two days' growth of heard, bad teeth.* (2)

Lee is an outcast who prefers the company of the snakes in the desert to that of other men. A virtual illiterate, he makes his living by theft. For Lee, the candlelight by which Austin works is reminiscent of the "old guys," "The Forefathers" (6). Most directly, the allusion is to the first settlers of the West, but the somewhat odd phrasing, the repetition, and the capitalization draw our attention to the masculinity of these Forefathers and may recall the Hebrew patriarchs. Like those patriarchs and like Abel, Lee is associated with the sacrifice of animals. In Scene 1 he brags to Austin: "Had me a Pit Bull there for a while but I lost him ... Fightin' dog. Damn I made some good money off that little dog. Real good money" (9).

In Genesis blood sacrifice is required by the patriarchal deity Yahweh, and in *True West* Lee is clearly allied with the masculine and violent values of this deity. Even Lee's vocabulary associates him with blood sacrifices. When Austin innocently offers to give him money, Lee furiously rejects the gift, calling it "Hollywood blood money" and accusing Austin of attempting to use that money to "buy off" the "Old Man" (8). Throughout much of the play, references to the father, who is (like the mother) left unnamed, prompt in Lee a sense of reverence and pride, while in Austin such references provoke an outbreak of hostility, guilt, or disgust. Thus, in the play, as in Genesis, the patriarchal and matriarchal systems clash.

In the Americanized mythology of *True West*, however, the biblical story of Cain and Abel undergoes ironic and comic revisions that undermine both the patriarchal values of Lee and the matriarchal values of Austin. The true American deity is Success, and Austin is initially that deity's favored child. The deity's agent is a Hollywood producer named Saul Kimmer, who has promised Austin a lucrative movie contract for the love story he is writing.

In contrast, Lee offers Saul a Western about a man's confrontation with his wife's lover and involving a bizarre chase in which two horses are taken by trailer to the Texas panhandle and then ridden into the desert at night. Lee seeks Austin's creative assistance in writing an outline of the plot, but he angrily rejects the notion that Austin's contribution is important or inspired: "Favor! Big Favor! Handin' down favors from the mountain top" (23). The implication is that Austin is not like God handing down the tablets to Moses; what Austin hands down, Lee is quite prepared to reject. Clichéd as Lee's story is, it holds out the promise of a bloody duel at the end, the blood offering that Abel presented to Yahweh. As one might predict, the god of Hollywood eventually rejects Austin's comparatively wholesome love story and smiles on Lee's Western, just as the Old Testament deity accepted Abel's blood sacrifice and threw down the altar of Cain.

NOTE

[3] Sam Shepard, *True West*, in *Sam Shepard: Seven Plays* (New York, 1981), 3. Subsequent page references to the play are to this edition and will appear in my text.

—Jeffrey D. Hoeper, "Cain, Canaanites, and Philistines in Sam Shepard's True West." *Modern Drama* 36, no. 1 (March 1993): 76, 77-79.

Fool for Love

Fool for Love was first performed at the Magic Theatre in San Francisco in 1983. Shepard wrote the screenplay for the movie version in 1985 and played the part of Eddie. The play revisits Shepard's interest in the theme of incest, though it is treated more lightly in this play, in the context of what Frank Rich called an "indoor rodeo." To the audience, Eddie and May first appear as lovers, but then it is revealed that they are half siblings. Their rough-and-tumble arguments, part of their peculiar intimacy, seem as much about sibling rivalry as they do about romantic love, as do their heated embraces. Shepard skillfully creates an energy between May and Eddie that merges sexual chemistry with familial affection, and lovers' jealousy with competition for a father's love. As is often the case with Shepard's family plays, the questions of identity return always to the absent father; thus remaining unanswered. Unlike in *True West* (1980), where the father is only accessible in memory, the Old Man in *Fool for Love* physically appears but is already dead and tells lies.

The play is meant to be "performed relentlessly without a break," and the setting is a "stark, low-rent motel room on the edge of the Mojave Desert." A platform is added on to the extreme down left edge of the stage, where the Old Man, an aged cowboy, sits on a rocker drinking whiskey out of a styrofoam cup. He exists in the minds of May and Eddie, sitting on the bed and at the table, respectively, but interacts with them as though he exists on their physical plane.

Eddie, a rodeo stuntman described as smelling of horse sweat and having a body that is "aged long before his time," begins a tediously circular conversation with May, his lover. In this lengthy exchange, Eddie tries to convince May that he will never leave her again and he has been faithful to her in his absence. Eddie believes he and May are meant to be together and wants to set up a trailer for their home. May, meanwhile, moves between desperately clinging to Eddie and snubbing him, expressing knowingly that he is not faithful to her and will most definitely leave, "erasing" her. Luring Eddie with a kiss, she knees him in the groin and goes into the bathroom to get ready for a date which she has planned for the evening.

The Old Man, Eddie's father, then attempts to teach his son about the difference between fantasy and realism. He points to a nonexistent picture of Barbara Mandrell and tells him that he is actually married to her in his mind—and that gives it the power of realism. Through the Old Man, Shepard may be calling attention to the act of representation and insinuating that the drama that will follow between Eddie and May will only take place in the Old Man's mind. But nothing is certain, and this resistance to dramatic resolution is one of Shepard's trademarks.

May comes back into the room and changes into a sexy red dress and heels. When Eddie finds out that May has a date, he leaves and comes back with a bottle of tequila and a shotgun, much like a jealous lover. May knows Eddie's game by now: as soon as she and Eddie are together for a little while, he will wander off. Eddie calls her a traitor for forgetting their "pact," reminding May that she will never be able to replace him. He storms out of the room, which causes May to weep while clinging to and moving along the wall. Shepard's stage direction requires that loud booms sound every time the doors close, so the booms that punctuate the lovers' arguments reflect the volatility not only of the relationship but the act of representing it.

The Old Man, who is also May's father, begins to tell a story of traveling with her and May's mother, in which he took May into a herd of mooing cattle in total darkness to stop her crying. May picks herself up out of her grief and begins drinking from Eddie's bottle, falling off the wagon again. Eddie enters and begins roping the bedposts as if he is in a rodeo. As he is doing this, they bicker: Eddie accuses May of fabricating her date, while at the same time vowing to "nail his ass to the floor" and backing the threat up by dragging a lassoed chair violently across the room. May is defensive of her suitor and calls Eddie a "jealous, little snot-nosed kid," threatening to leave. But she leaves the door open as she exits and Eddie follows her and carries her back in kicking and screaming. Here the two betray themselves as siblings, as they walk the fine line between filial play and sexual tension.

Suddenly a black Mercedes Benz pulls up outside the window

and May notices that a woman in the car is staring at her. A gunshot, shattered glass, and a blaring horn are heard offstage. May jealously identifies the woman in the car as the "countess," a name she uses to describe Eddie's rich paramour. Eddie realizes this woman has shot through the windshield of his truck and urges May to leave with him to avoid further danger. May's jealousy peaks, while Eddie insists the "countess" does not mean anything to him. May refuses to leave with Eddie, then both stand looking at each other while the Old Man muses that neither May nor Eddie carry any resemblance to him, only to their mothers. He is "totally unrecognizable" in them. As in much of Shepard's work, identity and family resemblance are often blurred, partly because family members can be strangers to each other, and because paternity is not always certain. The term "family" becomes arbitrary at best.

May's and Eddie's verbal dance begins again, and now both are drunk. Eddie vows that May will never get rid of him, and May complains that he has manipulated her for fifteen years. As headlights again shine from outside onto the stage, Eddie tries to force May into the bathroom but is met by shouts of protest, both at Eddie and the countess. Obviously concerned about the noise he hears, Martin, May's date, crashes through the door and pulls Eddie to the ground. May prevents Martin from hitting Eddie by telling him that it was just an argument. May invites Martin to have a drink and Eddie begins questioning Martin as both a protective brother and jealous ex-lover. He tells Martin that a lie is not a lie when you know it is not true, but that when you believe a lie to be true, it is lying.

Martin attempts to leave, but Eddie prevents him by pulling him out of the window by the back of his pants and slamming him against the wall. Eddie reveals to Martin that May is his half-sister. Their father lived alternately with each of their mothers, disappearing in between. While the Old Man interjects to revise points of Eddie's story, Eddie recounts to Martin the night he met May. His father took him on a long walk in silence. They drank a bottle of liquor together and ended up at the house of May's mother, in front of whom his father cried and cried. Eddie saw May appear and at first sight they both knew they would always love each other.

May calls Eddie a liar and continues the story her way. After May searches tirelessly for her father, who tried his best to keep his two lovers apart, her mother found him and she and May first saw Eddie through the window of his house while he ate dinner. Two weeks later, the old man vanished without a trace and while May's mother was grieving, May was falling deliriously in love. When May's mother begged Eddie's mother to get Eddie to stay away, Eddie's mother blew her brains out.

The Old Man then tells his own version of the story. May's mother was so persistent and openly enamoured of him that he could not resist her. The Old Man insists that Eddie back him up based on a pact the two have made. Eddie refuses, drawing closer to May and kissing her. The two lovers are so wrapped up in each other that they barely notice the loud collision, shattering glass, screaming horses, and fiery explosion caused by the countess returning with her wrath. Eddie eventually steps away from May and tells her he will be right back, but May tells Martin "he's gone" with a note of heavy finality. As Martin stares at the open door, and May exits with a packed suitcase, the Old Man points again at his nonexistent picture and insists that it holds the woman of his dreams, all his forever. The fire from the explosion burns outside as Martin watches it with his back to the audience and the old man rocks in his chair.

Fool for Love

May, in her early thirties, has spent her adult life chasing and escaping from the dream of continuing a love affair with her lover and half-brother Eddie. A transient, she cannot seem to move far enough away from Eddie, who has sought her out in a run-down motel in the Mojave Desert; nor can she get close enough to him. Like her mother, whose story she tells, May is obsessed with a man who lives a double life and has been alternately pursuing and fleeing her for fifteen years. Throughout the play, May enacts her own approach-avoidance by alternately clinging to Eddie, telling him to leave, and threatening to leave him. As the play nears its end, May finds herself abandoned again as Eddie leaves with the all-too-familiar "I'll come right back. Okay?" In response, she packs her suitcase to continue her transient life.

Eddie, in his late thirties, is May's half-brother and lover. He is a real cowboy, smelling of horse sweat and wearing duct tape around his boots. He is described as aged before his time, and this is not just because he has spent most of his time on a horse and drinks excessively. As the play bears out, Eddie is aged with the burden of his double life, just as his father was. He has both duplicated and assumed the burden of his father's sexual double-dealing, splitting himself between May and another woman. For most of the play, Eddie tries to win May back with vows of undying and singular affection, while sustaining serious damage to his car and trailer at the hands of the jealous other woman; but because of his history of disappearing, May remains unconvinced by his words. Despite May's cynicism and the forbidding haunting of his father (the Old Man), Eddie manages to spend a passionate moment with May before disappearing again.

The Old Man appears physically to the audience as an old cowboy in a rocking chair drinking whiskey, though he is really dead. Father to both May and Eddie, he speaks to them from the past, though only Eddie acknowledges him. When he was alive, he wandered restlessly between their mothers, never committing to either and apparently driving Eddie's mother to suicide. He provides a frame to the play, beginning it and ending it with reference to a nonexistent picture of Barbara Mandrell whom he claims is his wife. This framing is ultimately a theatrical device that keeps the audience away from a comfortable resolution about what is real and what is made up.

Martin is May's date for the evening. He shows up to a hysterical May wrangling with Eddie over his other lover and naively tries to save May by taking Eddie to the ground. Though he tries to keep a polite distance from Eddie's and May's squabble, he is drawn into it by them, functioning as the sounding board for Eddie's and May's conflicting versions of their past. At the end of the play, after both Eddie and May disappear, he can only stare out the motel room window, his back to the audience, as Eddie's trailer goes up in flames.

Fool for Love

FRANK RICH ON SHEPARD'S AUTHENTIC WESTERN VISION

[Frank Rich is an op-ed columnist for *The New York Times* and has also served as the paper's chief drama critic. He has written about culture and politics for many publications, including *Time, Esquire,* and *The New Republic*. In this excerpt, Rich compliments Shepard's ability to conjure up a lost American west before the audience's eyes.]

No one knows better than Sam Shepard that the true American West is gone forever, but there may be no writer alive more gifted at reinventing it out of pure literary air. Like so many Shepard plays, "Fool for Love," at the Circle Repertory Company, is a western for our time. We watch a pair of figurative gunslingers fight to the finish—not with bullets, but with piercing words that give ballast to the weight of a nation's buried dreams.

As theater, "Fool for Love" could be called an indoor rodeo. The setting is a present-day motel room on the edge of the Mojave Desert where for 90 minutes, May (Kathy Baker) and Eddie (Ed Harris) constantly batter one another against the walls. May and Eddie have been lovers for 15 years; they may even, like the fratricidal antagonists of "True West," be siblings. But May has had it: she'd now like nothing more than to "buffalo" Eddie by stabbing him in the middle of a passionate kiss.

Eddie is some sort of rancher, complete with saddle, rifle and lasso. Yet there's no more range—Marlboro men ride only on television—and he lives in a tin trailer. The motel room is May's most recent home. With its soiled green walls and a window facing black nothingness, it looks like a jail call; its doors slam shut with a fierce metallic clang. When Eddie uses his rope, all he can snare is a bedpost. When the two lovers want to escape, they don't mount horses for a fast getaway—they merely run to the parking lot and back.

But if the West is now reduced to this—a blank empty room with an unmade bed—Mr. Shepard fills that space with reveries as big as all outdoors. When the play's fighting lets up, we hear monologues resembling crackling campfire tales. The characters—who also include May's new suitor (Dennis Ludlow) and a ghostly "old man" (Will Marchetti) sipping Jim Beam in a rocking chair—try to find who they are and where they are. Though the West has become but a figment of the movies, Eddie contends "there's not a movie in this town that can match the story I can tell."

Laced with the floating images of cattle herds, old cars and even a spectral Spencer Tracy looming in the dark, these hallucinatory stories chart the Shepard vision. His characters are "disconnected"; they fear being "erased"; they hope to be "completely whole." In "Fool for Love," each story gives us a different "version" of who May, Eddie and the old man are, and the stories rarely mesh in terms of facts. Yet they do cohere as an expression of the author's consciousness: as Shepard's people race verbally through the debris of the West, they search for the identities and familial roots that have disappeared with the landscape of legend.

Not finding what they seek, they use their dreams as weapons, to wipe each other out. The old man, a ghostly figure who may be May and Eddie's father, tells the couple that they could be "anybody's children" "I don't recognize myself in either of you and never did." Eddie and May respond in kind, even as they obliterate their own shared past. "You got me confused with someone else," says May to her lover, vowing never again to be suckered into one of his "little fantasies." What remains of Eddie's fantastical West is ultimately destroyed, too: his few horses burn in the play's apocalyptic finale.

Mr. Shepard's conceits are arresting and funny. Eddie, in explaining his particular erotic fixation, tells May that her neck keeps "coming up for some reason." The old man contends he is married to Barbara Mandrell and announces, without much fear of contradiction, that the singer's picture is hanging on an empty wall. There is a strange poignancy to May's suitor, a gentle maintenance man too lost even to dream of a self. Like a much talked-about "countess" of Eddie's supposed acquaintance, this sweet gentleman caller, intentionally or not, provides "Fool for Love" with an odd, unlikely echo of Tennessee Williams.

The production at the Circle Rep allows New York audiences to see the play in its native staging. "Fool for Love" has been transported here from Mr. Shepard's home base, the Magic Theater of San Francisco, complete with the original cast under the author's direction. The actors are all excellent: With utter directness, they create their own elusive yet robust world—feisty, muscular, sexually charged—and we either enter it or not.

—Frank Rich, "Buffaloing Eddie." *The New York Times*, 26 May 1983. *The New York Times Theater Reviews* (1983-4): 88.

T.E. Kalem on Animal Combat and the War Between the Sexes

[T.E. Kalem has been a theater critic for *Time Magazine* and his witty prose has been included in *Simpson's Contemporary Quotations* (1988). In this excerpt, Kalem argues that the central theme of the play is "bloodlust" and can be seen in the animalistic square-offs between Eddie and May.]

In Sam Shepard's plays, human contact is animal combat. There is a surreal humor in the struggle, but, make no mistake, it is a struggle to the death.

In *True West*, two brothers resolve their differences in the exact manner of Cain and Abel. In *The Tooth of Crime*, two rock stars, Hoss and Crow, meet on the killing ground of the territorial imperative. Who shall be king? The play is like the jungle ritual in which the young lion destroys the old lion to become leader of the pride.

One might assume from the title that Shepard's latest play, *Fool for Love*, is devoted to that magnificent obsession known as romantic love. It is, in fact, a peripheral theme. But the core of this drama is lust and blood lust. The war between the sexes is not remotely related to quibbling matches about who does the dishes and who changes the diapers. Indeed, Shepard's family plays, *Buried Child*, for which he won the Pulitzer Prize in 1979, and *Curse of the Starving Class*, display no traces of cozy domesticity. There is only the baleful sense of wary enemies endlessly circling and stalking each other, waiting to deliver, or receive, an invisible dagger thrust. In *Fool for Love*, the lovers, Eddie (Ed Harris) and May (Kathy Baker), are locked in a struggle for absolute power.

They have been lovers for 15 years, and they have punched quite a bit of hate into the affair. Periodically. Eddie has cut out on a freedom binge but has always returned to exact sexual fealty from May. This is another reunion in a dingy motel room on the edge of the Mojave Desert. In a malignant fury over Eddie's having bedded some shadowy "countess," May resolves that it is time to say goodbye for keeps. She rants and rails and Eddie pleads and storms, but each time one threatens to go, the other extends the battle with an imperious command or a passion pitch of need.

Even the love play is ominous. At one point, Eddie and May are all over each other in a steamy clinch at the end of which she knees him in the groin. With his cowboy spurs and boots—Shepard's symbols for the untrammeled, virile male—Eddie hurls himself against walls, somersaults across the floor and swings his lariat to rope in bedposts and random chairs. This is an amusing form of sexual intimidation, but it does not wholly evade silliness. It works best in a macho-*vs.*-mouse encounter between Eddie and the gentleman caller (Dennis Ludlow) who has come to take May to a movie.

In an effort to give a vivid but scarcely mind-churning work more mythic gravity, Shepard makes known along the way that the lovers are half sister and half brother. Somehow this lacks impact, merely suggesting that incest is the most potent brand of sibling rivalry. In the cast at off-Broadway's Circle Repertory Company, Ed Harris invests Eddie with the driving electric intensity of a younger Robert Duvall, and Kathy Baker's May is a scorchy spitfire.

—T.E. Kalem, "The Theater: Bloodlust," *Time Magazine* (6 June 1983). *New York Theatre Critics' Reviews* (1983): 215.

STEVEN PUTZEL ON THE SHOCK VALUE OF THE PLAY

[Steven Putzel is a Professor of Liberal Arts at The Pennsylvania State University Wilkes-Barre campus. In this excerpt from *Modern Drama*, Putzel argues that the play's spectator-assaulting effects warp traditional theatrical space and challenge the audience to be complicit in the production.]

Fool for Love, as interpreted under Shepard's own direction, is another attempt to find new chords and it demands a very different complicity with the audience. This play, with its solid, kettle-drum walls, refuses to allow the audience to remain in safety. Though stopping short of Handke's insulting of the audience, this play approaches Artaud's assault on them. What has happened between 1976 and 1983 is that Shepard is now a familiar figure to the mid-town New York audience, an audience that he himself has helped to create. Still there is mystery, still there is audience anticipation and confutation, and still there are multiplaned or multi-dimensional acting spaces. The audience is confronted by the violent emotions that hurl Eddie and May around the motel room, against the walls and into the locked bathroom located just off-stage right. Each time Eddie throws himself against the wall the audience cringes, not because there is a slice of life before them, but because they feel threatened by the loud sound. Spectators also recognize an off-stage world of violence represented by the arcing headlights, the "sound of loud collision, shattering glass, an explosion" and the "Bright orange and blue light of a gasoline fire [that] suddenly illuminates [the] upstage window" (*Fool*, p. 55). The raw emotion, the primal passion, the constant imminence of physical violence momentarily shock spectators out of their comfort and force a more than aesthetic involvement.

Although the audience is forced to be more directly involved, more deeply complicit in *Fool for Love* than it has been in earlier plays, Shepard does not "open" his stage to allow Brechtian actor-to-audience communication nor does he allow the character –audience communication of a Shakespearian soliloquy. Yet, as in *Suicide in B^b*, he avoids naturalism's fiction of a completely closed stage and he violates the fourth wall convention by creating what is in effect a fifth wall.[9] The Old Man who rocks downstage left speaks from a different time and place, talking and even walking through the fourth wall. He is a ghostly witness to May and Eddie's opening lines, he delivers the final words of the play, and he rocks in his chair alone as the lights fade. Unlike the familiar expressionistic convention of memory flashbacks, such as those experienced by Willie Loman in *Death of a Salesman*, the Old Man's conversations with Eddie leave the audience unable to define clearly the time and place from which he speaks. He may be a projection from Eddie's thoughts, or a manifestation of Shepard's father–son fixation, conveying his presumed assumption that genetic memory is carried only by Y chromosomes, for May never acknowledges the Old Man's presence.

Modern audiences should be accustomed to dealing with figurative space–time warps, but Shepard's use of these warps is proxemic or theatrical rather than merely rhetorical; we have to decide how to respond to the Old Man's physical presence. Until midway through the play he is confined to his stage-left platform, and so we are able to explain him away as a manifestation of Eddie's torment over his and May's incestuous infatuation. Suddenly the imaginary wall that the audience had constructed separating the main acting space and the platform is breached when the Old Man reaches on stage to allow Eddie to pour him a glass of tequila, and again when he excitedly stands, leaves his platform and comes on stage to stand between May and Eddie. This is Shepard's rather unsubtle method of signifying by a physical barrier, the social taboo, the common paternity that turns their passion to tragedy.

As both the cause and the physical manifestation of the tension between May and Eddie, the Old Man serves a central thematic and theatrical function. As a character speaking from an indeterminate space and time, the Old Man also serves a meta-theatrical function; he prevents the audience from identifying the play as "Realism." At the beginning of the play he incongruously asks Eddie "would you believe me if I told ya' I was married to [Barbara Mandrell]?" After Eddie answers a simple "No," the Old Man responds "Well, see, now that's the difference right there. That's realism. I am actually married to Barbara Mandrell in my mind. Can you understand that?" (*Fool*, p. 27). This acts as a warning to the audience, letting us know that there are different planes of reality, different levels of "truths" and "lies," and that we will need to expand our expectations beyond realism in order to become complicit in the performance.

In each of the texts and productions discussed thus far, Shepard is certainly not pandering to public taste or making it easy for the audience to "understand," or in Pavis's words, to interpret his work naively. Instead he seemed content with the small but extremely receptive audiences of San Francisco's Magic Theatre and New York's off-Broadway houses, audiences who, with their willingness to expand their expectations and to become complicit in the production, have encouraged experimentation and innovation.

NOTE

9 In "Double Jeopardy," an interview with Adrian Hall by Arthur Bartow in *American Theatre*, 2 (1986), 10–17, Hall discusses his experience directing *Fool for Love* in Dallas and provides an informative note to this discussion of "open" and "closed" stages. He explains that after listening aghast to Eddie's first few speeches gray-haired spectators would get up and leave. Finally, Richard Jenkins, the actor playing Eddie, pointed his shot gun at a pair of these sensitive spectators keeping them in his sights until they came to the top of the aisle. Suddenly another spectator yelled "Pull the trigger!" This Brechtian "stage-opening" action caused the house to break up in laughter, but, since the play does not depend on the naturalistic fiction of the closed stage, the production continued unharmed and perhaps enhanced.

> —Steven Putzel, "Expectation, Confutation, Revelation: Audience Complicity in the Plays of Sam Shepard." *Modern Drama* 30, no. 2 (June 1987): 155-156.

DAVID J. DEROSE ON SHEPARD'S NEW CONSERVATISM

[David J. DeRose's essays on Sam Shepard have appeared in *Theater, American Theatre,* and *Theatre Journal*. In this excerpt, DeRose compares the conventional restraint of the play ("new" Shepard) with Shepard's earlier, more intuitive style ("old" Shepard).]

In spite of the work in both theater and film that Shepard has done since *Fool for Love*, it is difficult not to see this play as the culmination of his career as a dramatist to date. Director Jacques Levy once said of Shepard's early work that "Sam is more interested in *doing* something to audiences than in saying something to them" (Levy, 98). With *Fool for Love*, Shepard fulfills the intention of "doing something" to his audience; that is, he reaches the audience on a visceral level with the play's ambiguous dreamlike setting and with its fierce expressionistic staging. But the achievement of *Fool for Love* is that it works not only on this theatrical level but also on a dramatic and thematic level as well. *Fool for Love* both does something to the audience and tells them something at the same time. It successfully blends form and content, creating a theatrical spectacle of juxtaposed realities that embodies the play's thematic preoccupation with illusion and the subjectivity of reality.

The irony of Shepard's achievement in *Fool for Love* is that it seems to have been accomplished almost against his will. Shepard has said in numerous interviews that he wrote as many as 16 drafts of *Fool for Love* before he felt he had a play that remained true to the realistically drawn lovers and their naturalistically pitched situation.[22] What Shepard does not mention in those interviews is that it was not until the final draft of the play that he introduced the spectral presence of the old man into the script.[23] Until that draft, the play had been a conventional romantic confrontation between the long-separated lovers, Eddie and May. That Shepard would write well over a dozen drafts of a realistic play, and then finally complete a satisfactory draft only after the inspired addition of the old man, suggests the power of Shepard's intuitive theatricality over his conscious attempts to write within the self-imposed restraints of psychological realism. The solution to Shepard's writing problem was not a psychological or dramatic one but a theatrical one, involving the presence of a character who suspends the play between fantasy and reality.

The struggle between the "old" Shepard's theatrical intuition and the "new" Shepard's conscious restraint can be further felt in the published text of *Fool for Love*. In that text, Shepard states that the old man "exists only in the minds of MAY and EDDIE" (*FFL*, 15). This rationalization of the old man's presence would have been totally unnecessary for the "old" Sam Shepard, who felt perfectly comfortable with intersecting planes of reality in *Suicide in B-Flat*. As noted earlier, when *Fool for Love* is performed live, there is no suggestion in the play itself that the old man is being imagined or dreamed by either Eddie or May. In fact, one has the distinct impression on several occasions, especially at the end of the play when May and Eddie have both left the stage, that the old man may well be dreaming them. And yet Shepard felt obliged, when publishing the play, to rationalize the old man's existence.

While many reviewers, including myself,[24] wished to see *Fool for Love* as the final triumphant resurrection of the "old" Shepard in a new glorious incarnation as an innovative family dramatist, the inclusion of this single stage direction in the text of the play should have served as a sobering indicator of the conservative direction Shepard's career was continuing to take in spite of *Fool for Love*. He has since rejected anything about his family plays that "smacks of the 'old' Shepard," citing examples of suprareal and surreal staging from *Curse of the Starving Class*, *Buried Child*, and *Fool for Love* as sources of embarrassment (Allen, 150). Shepard's most recent family play is the sadly conventional, tamely self-imitative *A Lie of the Mind*.

NOTES

[22] Shepard discusses the composition of *Fool for Love* in Lippman and in Jennifer Allen, "The Man on the High Horse: On the Trail of Sam Shepard," *Esquire*, November 1988, 141–44, et passim; hereafter cited in text.

[23] A draft of the script dated only "1982," which I read in the offices of the Magic Theatre in San Francisco, has no old man in it. The final draft of the script, used in production, was dated "12/82." Advance publicity from the Magic Theatre, which appeared in the spring of 1982, announced that Shepard's new play would have "two men and two women"—that is, Eddie, May, Martin, and the countess. In John Lion's *American Theatre* article, he also makes reference to the fact that he auditioned "about a hundred actresses" for the role of the princess" before Shepard ever showed him a draft of the script. That draft; which Lion estimates was number 11, had no "princess" and no old man. See John Lion, "Rock 'n Roll Jesus with a Cowboy Mouth," *American Theatre* 1 (April 1984), 6.

[24] See David J. DeRose, "*Fool for Love*" [theatre review], *Theatre Journal* 36 (March 1984), 100–101.

> —David J. DeRose, *Sam Shepard*, (New York: Twayne Publishers, 1992): 121-123.

MARTIN TUCKER ON DUAL OPPOSITION AND ITS INDIVIDUAL AND EPIC DIMENSIONS

[Martin Tucker is the editor of *Literary Exile in the Twentieth Century: An Analysis and Biographical Dictionary* (1991). In this excerpt, Tucker explores the theme of unresolved conflict on the individual and the epic level.]

Shepard had achieved a certain measure of happiness in his meeting with Jessica Lange by 1982, and he had become a major film star as a result of his role in *The Right Stuff*. He continued to work with the Magic Theatre in San Francisco, where he had achieved a second success after his self-exile in England. In *Fool for Love*, first produced at the Magic Theatre on February 8, 1983, with Shepard directing and the two lead roles played by Kathy Baker and Ed Harris, Shepard objectified his search for passage through experience to a measure of maturity. The play moved to New York in May 1983 and had a long and popular run at the Circle Repertory Company. It was made into a movie, with Shepard playing the lead role of Eddie; Shepard also wrote the screenplay for director Robert Altman.

In plot sequence the play is a narrative of two lovers—one a cowboy stunt man who has been injured enough physically to walk on a permanent limp-line through life but whose spirit refuses to die; the other is his half-sister, whose passion for her lover-sibling refuses as well to die. They leave each other, find each other, kick each other, and never forget each other. In the short span of time in which the play unfolds its dramatic action, Eddie has traveled more than a thousand miles to see Mae, who has run away from him and now lives in a dumpy motel. Mae works as a waitress and is supposedly on the way to starting a new life without Eddie. When Eddie shows up, she rejects his advances verbally and physically; at the same time she holds onto the line of contact between them. Two rivals, one for Eddie, one for Mae, are in the background. Eddie has a countess in a Mercedes Benz waiting outside the motel room; she has followed Eddie in his thousand-mile trip. The premise is absurd (a millionaire countess obsessed with a broken-down, overage cowboy), but it makes for good fun and continues one of Shepard's appealing fantasies for men: that of being pursued as sexual object. (...)

Mae's story is quite different from Eddie's, but one father is inalterable: the father is the father is the father. Mae and Eddie are thus joined—by blood, by passion, by a tie they cannot unbind. The father, speaking on the sidelines of the stage action, demands that Eddie stand up for him and declare that the father met his responsibilities, that the father's marriage with his legal wife was an impossibility to uphold, and that he, the father, has his "rights." As all the monologues unfold, the gentle Martin and swain of Mae, who knows very little of Mae's past, attempts some synthesis of the passionate, swirling stories. Martin is the steady sod of the earth (he has just watered it before coming to pick up Mae), while Eddie and

Mae are the transients of the desert; like the sand grains, they blow from one place to another, they explode and fly away on the wind. Indeed, Eddie leaves the scene with the countess in her car, and Mae packs a bag as Martin watches her in stupefied amazement. In the final moment of the play the spotlight turns on the father—whom the stage directions indicate is a construct of Eddie's and Mae's consciousness. They talk to him, but he is *not* there. Or is he, if they believe he is there? The father, in the same manner, says at the conclusion of the play that he is looking at a picture of the woman of his dreams, but there is no picture on the wall he is looking at. The will is empty, except for the imagination of it.

The success of *Fool for Love* is the result of many qualities. The play is a rollicking feast of passion. Eddie and Mae go at and after each other in a nonstop, dizzying fashion that delights by its sheer energy and by its amazingly inventive feats of obstinacy. The dream—or imagination—sequences with the old man/father figure have a poignancy and a clarity not as easily obtainable in other Shepard plays. And the theme is romantic as possible, at least for Shepard, for it is a tale of young lovers, Romeo and Juliet escapees from warring families with the same father. Although the lovers are not capable of lasting commitment because they will not drop their option of future alternatives, they are enveloped in the presence of an overwhelming passion, a presence that suggests a kind of crazy hope for their future. For even if Eddie runs off with the countess, a move that can only insure his transience one more time, he has the lasting image of Mae to sustain his possibilities. Although Mae says good-bye to the steadiness of the stolid nice guy, Martin, she too is not completely bereft; she has her image of Eddie to sustain her, even if the sustenance comes from throwing darts into his cardboard image. The play is reassuring on this note as well as on the note of the father's dream making, or the imagination of how things can be made to seem. Eddie and Mac's resilience suggest that Shepard in this play has moved beyond the knots that prevented action, even the action of flight, in some of his earlier work. Eddie is running away, but he is running, he has movement in his life. Mae is moving as well, even if her life from town to town seems tawdry and boringly repetitive. While maturity is not on their doorstep, it may be around some corner. At the least, Mac and Eddie have the limbs to find its branches (even with Eddie's limp). The two lovers have not lost their chances at life, and the old man has resigned himself to his imagination as his soul and sole companion. *Fool for Love* becomes Shepard's least-troubled play in its comedy of passionate foolishness as well as foolish passion. The imagination of it—that is, their imagination of their capabilities—enables them to love and leave each other.

It seems of some lingering significance that Shepard left his wife O-Lan after the opening of *Fool for Love* and joined in a union with Jessica Lange. Shepard's plays are often "departures" (the word has been used by various friends of Shepard when they describe events Shepard has taken from their lives) from the premise of a real, biographical situation. His newest play and his real-life act of marital separation for a new union of love suggest that *Fool for Love* is a valentine for what-has-been and an appreciation of both the past and the possible future.

—Martin Tucker, *Sam Shepard*, (New York: The Continuum Publishing Company, 1992): 119-123

SHERRILL GRACE ON THE PLAY'S EXPRESSIONISTIC STAGING

[Sherrill Grace is the author of *Margaret Atwood: Language, Text, and System* (1983) and *Regression and Apocalypse: Studies in North American Literary Expressionism* (1989) and the editor of *Staging The North: Twelve Canadian Plays* (1999). In this excerpt, Grace argues that Shepard's use of color, sound and non-linear narrative make it an excellent example of expressionism.]

An expressionist poetics enables the writer to articulate a vision that is seldom pretty or comforting. Literary and cultural historians have argued that the rise of Expressionism in Germany in the first quarter of this century was intimately connected with the rise of fascism, and it is impossible to overlook the obsession with murder and power or the pervasive patriarchal violence (sons against fathers, males against females) in expressionist work or to deny the sense of crisis, alienation and collapse that is integral to the movement. At the same time, expressionist art, however muddled in its political message, was an art of protest against the cultural and spiritual bankruptcy of the times, against the horror of war and the capitalist and military agenda of the German state. The artist's nostalgic retreat from such a world into nature or within the territory of his own Soul was not an effective political strategy then and it probably will not be now, but perhaps that is not the point. The expressionist vision brings us face to face with a terrible human cry of terror and warning, a cry that can be heard in O'Neill, Glaspel, Williams and Kennedy, and that echoes through Shepard's work to climax in Beth's shattering scream: 'WHO FELL ME!!!'[4] (...)

However straightforward they may seem at first, however careful Shepard may be about realistic details or with characters who seem very familiar, sooner or later an audience is forced to abandon the comfortable realm of logic, clarity, predictability and familiarity for an illogical realm of intense emotion, violent unpredictability and complex symbolic, inner states. And it is at precisely that point, that taut moment, that border between the real and the symbolic, but where both are fully at play, that Expressionism lives. (...)

Buried Child, *True West*, and *Fool for Love* all function through nonlinear, dislocated structures. In each there is a clear thread of plot, of narrative progression from beginning to middle to abrupt end, but it is not this horizontal movement that controls the dramatic action or gives rise to the acute tension in each play. Instead, each develops vertically through a centripetal accumulation of repeated, but basically similar moments which, in the end, return the characters to the same position they were in at the beginning—albeit in states of greater loss (*Curse*), heightened confusion and despair (*Buried Child*), deeper hostility (*True West*) or a more acute alienation and withdrawal (*Fool for Love* and *A Lie of the Mind*). (...)

Shepard has said that he dislikes resolutions in the theatre because he finds them false, and in the place of resolution Shepard offers, time and time again, images of violent (and purposeless) apocalypse, or of exhausted (and profoundly ambiguous) regression.[7] This opting for apocalyptic destruction or various forms of regressive withdrawal is typical of expressionist art which, by the basic nature of its enterprise, denies the possibility of alternative compromise positions or images of catharsis, let alone harmonious resolutions. (...)

Among the more recent plays, *Fool for Love* provides the most sustained and effective example of expressionist staging. Even before the lights begin to rise slowly on stage in the tempo of Merle Haggard's song 'Wake Up', the audience has entered the private world of May and Eddie, an impoverished, second-hand world of 'faded' and tired objects where the predominant colour is yellow—yellow table and chairs, a faded yellow exterior door, a yellow bathroom door standing slightly ajar to allow 'a yellow light to bleed onto stage' and a yellow-orange light from a streetlamp outside that shines through the window. Apart from the familiar, conventional association of the colour yellow with jealousy and cowardice, and the obvious relevance of these qualities to the inner lives of the characters, the yellow light establishes a disturbing, unnatural atmosphere right from the start. This atmosphere is further intensified by the 'weird stretching sound' Eddie makes with the bucking strap and by the doors and booming walls which Eddie and May continually slam or strike up against as they circle the room and each other. The Old Man, their father, located in his rocking chair on a small black platform stage left, 'exists only in the minds of Eddie and May', a fine example of expressionist literalised metaphor. Like the entire stage, he is a projection of what most haunts and cripples Eddie and May; he is both within them (in their minds, their genes, their past) and outside them, an expression in physical form of the social and cultural failure of contemporary life. Indeed, I would go further to say that, as the father, he symbolises a wide range of spiritual, psychological and ideological problems in Shepard's world.

The fact that *Fool for Love* must be 'performed relentlessly without a break' is the ultimate reminder that we are, for the duration exposed to the raw, tormented despair and conflict within two human souls. To the degree that we can connect emotionally with these people, recognising in them not so much a pair of representative, contemporary Americans but our own spiritual anguish and psychological crippling (simultaneously a desire for the object and a rejection of it), it is Shepard's tense balancing between abstraction and empathy, his expressionist staging that makes that recognition possible.

NOTES

[4] Though grammatically a question, Shepard punctuates Beth's cry as an extreme exclamation; see *A Lie of the Mind* (New York: New American Library, 1986), p. 5. All quotations are from this edition; page numbers are given in the text.

[7] In his interview with Amy Lippman, 'Rhythm and Truths', *American Theatre* 1, no. 1 (1984), Shepard says that he thinks 'it's a cheap trick to resolve things. It's a complete lie to make resolutions' (10), but resolution does not necessarily entail contrivance, and violent apocalypse or exhausted regression do not necessarily signify honesty.

> —Sherrill Grace, "Lighting Out for the Territory Within: Field Notes on Shepard's Expressionist Vision." *Rereading Shepard: Contemporary Critical Essays on the Plays of Sam Shepard*, ed. Leonard Wilcox (New York: St. Martin's Press, 1993): 182-183, 184, 185, 187-188.

Sam Shepard

Cowboys. 1964.

The Rock Garden. 1964.

Up to Thursday. 1964.

Chicago. 1965.

Dog. 1965.

4-H Club. 1965.

Icarus' Mother. 1965.

Rocking Chair. 1965.

Fourteen Hundred Thousand. 1966.

Red Cross. 1966.

Cowboys #2. 1967.

Five Plays: Chicago, Icarus' Mother, Red Cross, Fourteen Hundred Thousand, Melodrama Play. 1967.

Forensic and the Navigators. 1967.

La Turista. 1967.

Melodrama Play. 1967.

Fourteen Hundred Thousand (television). 1969.

Me and My Brother (screenplay, with Robert Frank). 1969.

The Holy Ghostly. 1969.

The Unseen Hand. 1969.

Operation Sidewinder. 1970.

Shaved Splits. 1970.

Zabriskie Point (screenplay, with Michelangelo Antonioni, Tonino Guerra, Fred Gardner and Clare Peploe). 1970.

Back Bog Beast Bait. 1971.

Cowboy Mouth. 1971.

Mad Dog Blues. 1971.

Ringaleerio. 1971.

Mad Dog Blues and Other Plays. 1971.

The Unseen Hand and Other Plays. 1971.

Blue Bitch (television play). 1972.

Oh! Calcutta! (screenplay, with others). 1972.

The Tooth of Crime. 1972.

Hawk Moon. 1973.

Nightwalk (with Megan Terry and Jean-Claude van Itallie). 1973.

Action. 1974.

Geography of a Horse Dreamer. 1974.

Little Ocean. 1974.

The Tooth of Crime and Geography of a Horse Dreamer. 1974.

Action and The Unseen Hand. 1975.

"Azusa Is a Real Place." In *Action and the Unseen Hand.* 1975.

Killer's Head. 1975.

Angel City. 1976.

Angel City and Other Plays. 1976.

Curse of the Starving Class. 1976.

The Sad Lament of Pecos Bill on the Eve of Killing His Wife. 1976.

Suicide in B Flat. 1976.

Inacoma. 1977.

Rolling Thunder Logbook. 1977.

"Visualization, Language, and the Inner Library." In *Drama
    Review* 21 (December 1977).

"American Experimental Theatre: Then and Now" (contributor). In
    Performing Arts Journal 2 (Fall 1977).

Buried Child. 1978.

Jacaranda (monologue). 1978.

Red Woman (monologue). 1978.

Renaldo and Clara (screenplay, with Bob Dylan). 1978.

Seduced. 1978.

"Time." In *Theater* Spring 1978.

Tongues (with Joseph Chaikin and others). 1978.

Buried Child and Other Plays. 1979.

Savage/Love (with Joseph Chaikin and others). 1979.

Buried Child and Seduced and Suicide in B-Flat. 1980.

Four Two-Act Plays. 1980.

Jackson's Dance (with Jacques Levy). 1980.

True West. 1980.

Chicago and Other Plays. 1981.

Seven Plays. 1981.

Motel Chronicles. 1982.

Fool for Love. 1983.

Fool for Love and The Sad Lament of Pecos Bill on the Eve of Killing His Wife. 1983.

Fool for Love and Other Plays. 1984.

Paris, Texas (screenplay). 1984.

True West (television). 1984.

A Lie of the Mind. 1985.

Fool for Love (screenplay). 1985.

The War in Heaven (radio play). 1985.

"True Dylan." In *Esquire* July 1987.

Far North (screenplay and direction). 1988.

Hawk Moon. 1989.

Joseph Chaikin and Sam Shepard: Letters and Texts, 1972-1984. 1989.

States of Shock. 1991.

Silent Tongue (screenplay and direction). 1992.

States of Shock, Far North, Silent Tongue. 1993.

Curse of the Starving Class (screenplay, with Bruce Beresford). 1994.

Simpatico: A Play in Three Acts. 1994.

Cruising Paradise: Tales. 1996.

Plays: 3. 1996.

When the World Was Green (with Joseph Chaikin). 1996.

Plays: 2. 1997.

Eyes for Consuela (based on *The Blue Bouquet* by Octovio Paz).
   1998.

The Late Henry Moss. 2000.

Great Dream of Heaven. 2002.

WORKS ABOUT

Sam Shepard

Adler, Thomas P. "Ghosts of Ibsen in Shepard's *Buried Child*." *Notes on Modern American Literature* 10, no. 1 (1986 Spring-Summer): 3.

Auerbach, Doris. *Sam Shepard, Arthur Kopit, and the Off Broadway Theater*. Boston: Twayne, 1982.

Benet, Carol. *Sam Shepard on the German Stage: Critics, Politics, Myths*. New York: Peter Lang, 1993.

Bloom, Clive, ed. *American Drama*. New York: St. Martin's Press, 1995.

Bock, Hedwig, and Wertheim, Albert, eds. *Essays on Contemporary American Drama*. Munich: M. Hueber, 161-172.

Bottoms, Stephen J. *The Theatre of Sam Shepard: States of Crisis*. Cambridge, England: Cambridge UP, 1998.

Callens, Johan. *From Middleton and Rowley's Chageling to Sam Shepard's Bodyguard: A Contemporary Appropriation of a Renaissance Drama*. Lewiston, NY: Edwin Mellen Press, 1997.

Canby, Vincent. "No Life in Antonioni's Death Valley." *The New York Times*, 13 February 1970. *The New York Times Film Reviews* (1969-1970): 133-134.

———. "Zabriskie Point." *The New York Times*, 10 February 1970. *The New York Times Film Reviews* (1969-1970): 131.

Clifton, Michael. "The Dark Vision of Shepard's *Buried Child*." *Journal of Evolutionary Psychology* 11, no. 1-2 (March 1990): 75-83.

Cohn, Ruby. "Portrait of the Artist as a Young Musician, Writer, Actor." *Contemporary Theatre Review: An International Journal* 8, no. 3 (1993): 67-77.

Daniel, Lanelle. "Ties of Blood: The Woman's Curse in Sam Shepard's Family Trilogy." *Publications of the Mississippi Philological Association* (1990): 129-133.

DeRose, David. *Sam Shepard*. New York: Twayne Publishers, 1992.

Demastes, William, Ed. *Realism and the American Dramatic Tradition.* Tuscaloosa, Alabama: University of Alabama Press, 1996.

Eder, Richard. "Stage: Sam Shepard Offers *Buried Child.*" *The New York Times,* 7 November 1978. In *New York Theatre Critics' Reviews* (1978): 146.

Giorcelli, Cristina, and Kroes, Rob, eds. *Living With America, 1946-1996.* Amsterdam, The Netherlands: VU University Press, 1997.

Goldstein, Richard. "Did Antonioni Miss the 'Point'?" *The New York Times,* 22 February 1970. In *The New York Times Film Reviews* (1969-1970): 137-138.

Gussow, Mel. "Brothers and Rivals." *The New York Times,* 18 October 1982. In *The New York Times Theater Reviews* (1981-2): 401-402.

―――. "Prodigal Grandson." *The New York Times,* 25 January 1979. In *The New York Times Theater Reviews* (1979-80): 15.

Hall, Ann C. *"A Kind of Alaska": Women in the Plays of O'Neill, Pinter and Shepard.* Illinois: Southern Illinois University Press, 1993.

Hart, Lynda. *Sam Shepard's Metaphorical Stages.* New York: Greenwood Press, 1987.

Hartigan, Karelisa V., ed. *From the Bard to Broadway.* Lanham, Maryland: University Press of America, 1987.

Hoeper, Jeffrey D. "Cain, Canaanites, and Philistines in Sam Shepard's *True West.*" *Modern Drama* 36, no. 1 (1993): 76-82.

Kalem, T.E. "The Theater: Bloodlust." *Time Magazine* (6 June 1983). *New York Theatre Critics' Reviews* (1983): 215.

King, Kimball, ed. *Sam Shepard: A Casebook.* New York: Garland Publishing, Inc., 1988.

Kroll, Jack. "California Dreaming," *Newsweek,* 5 January 1981. *New York Theatre Critics' Reviews* (1981): 367-368.

Malkin, Jeanette R. *Memory-Theater and Postmodern Drama.* Ann Arbor, MI: University of Michigan Press, 1999.

Marranca, Bonnie, ed. *American Dreams: The Imagination of Sam Shepard.* New York: *Performing Arts Journal Publications,* 1981.

McDonough, Carla. "The Politics of Stage Space: Women and Male Identity in Sam Shepard's Family Plays." *Journal of Dramatic Theory and Criticism* 9, no. 2 (1995 Spring); 65-83.

McGhee, Jim. *True Lies: The Architecture of the Fantastic in the Plays of Sam Shepard*. New York: Peter Lang, 1993.

Mogen, David, Sanders, Scott, and Karpinski, Joanne B., eds. *Frontier Gothic: Terror and Wonder at the Frontier in American Literature*. Rutherford, NJ: Fairleigh Dickinson UP, 1993.

Mottram, Ron. *Inner Landscapes: The Theater of Sam Shepard*. Columbia: University of Missouri Press, 1984.

Orbison, Tucker. "Mythic Levels in Shepard's *True West.*" *Modern Drama* 27, no. 4 (1984 December): 506-519.

Orr, John. *Tragicomedy and Contemporary Culture: Play and Performance from Beckett to Shepard*. Hampshire, Scotland: Macmillan, 1991.

Oumano, Ellen. *Sam Shepard: The Life and Work of an American Dreamer*. New York: St. Martin's Press, 1986.

Parker, Dorothy, ed. *Essays on Modern American Drama: Williams, Miller, Albee, and Shepard*. Toronto: University of Toronto Press, 1987.

Patraka, Vivian M., and Siegal, Mark. *Sam Shepard*. Boise, Idaho: Boise State University Press, 1985.

Peterson, Jane T. "Psychic Geography in *True West.*" *Notes on Contemporary Literature* 23, no. 1 (1993 January): 5-7.

Putzel, Steven. "Expectation, Confutation, Revelation: Audience Complicity in the Plays of Sam Shepard." *Modern Drama* 30, no. 2 (June 1987): 147-160.

Rabillard, Sheila. "Sam Shepard: Theatrical Power and American Dreams." *Modern Drama* 30, no. 1 (1987 March): 58-71.

Redmond, James, ed. *Violence in Drama*. Cambridge: Cambridge UP, 1991.

Rich, Frank. "Buffaloing Eddie." *The New York Times*, 26 May 1983. *The New York Times Theater Reviews* (1983-4): 88.

———. "Myth vs. Reality." *The New York Times*, 24 December 1980. In *The New York Times Theater Reviews* (1979-80): 456.

Schvey, Henry I. "A Worm in the Wood: The Father-Son Relationship in the Plays of Sam Shepard." *Modern Drama* 36, 1 (March 1993): 12 –26.

Schlueter, June, ed. *Feminist Rereadings of Modern American Drama*. Rutherford, NJ: Fairleigh Dickinson UP, 1989.

Siegel, Mark. "Holy Ghosts: The Mythic Cowboy in the Plays of Sam Shepard." *Bulletin of the Rocky Mountain Modern Language Association* 36, no. 4 (1982): 235-246.

Simard, Rodney. "American Gothic: Sam Shepard's Family Trilogy." *Theatre Annual: A Journal of Performance Studies* 41 (1986): 21-36.

Su, Tsu-chung. "The Double in Sam Shepard's *Buried Child* and *True West.*" *Studies in Language and Literature* 8 (1998 December): 65-83.

Taav, Michael. *A Body Across the Map: The Father-Son Plays of Sam Shepard*. New York: Peter Lang, 2000.

Tucker, Martin. *Sam Shepard*. New York: The Continuum Publishing Company, 1992.

Villella, Fiona A. "Here Comes the Sun: New Ways of Seeing in Antonioni's *Zabriskie Point.*" In Senses of Cinema (issue no. 4) [online journal]. Melbourne, Australia [cited March 2000]. Available from www.sensesofcinema.com. INTERNET.

Wade, Leslie. *Sam Shepard and the American Theatre*. Westport, Connecticut: Greenwood Press, 1997.

Westbrook, Max, and Flores, Dan, eds. *Updating the Literary West*. Fort Worth, TX: Western Literature Association and Texas Christian UP, 1997.

Wilcox, Leonard, ed. *Rereading Shepard: Contemporary Critical Essays on the Plays of Sam Shepard*. New York: St. Martin's Press, 1993.

Williams, Megan. "Nowhere Man and the Twentieth-Century Cowboy: Images of Identity and American History in Sam Shepard's *True West.*" *Modern Drama* 40, no. 1 (1997 Spring): 57-73.

Wright, Will, and Kaplan, Steve, eds. *The Image of the American West in Literature, The Media, and Society*. Pueblo, CO: Society for the Interdisciplinary Study of Social Imagery, University of Southern Colorado, 1996.

Yim, Harksoon. "Sam Shepard's Anti-Dialectics in *True West*." *Publications of the Mississippi Philological Association* (1998): 80-86.

Zinman, Toby Silverman. "Sam Shepard and Super-Realism." *Modern Drama* 29, no. 3 (1986 September): 423-430.

ACKNOWLEDGMENTS

"No Life in Antonioni's Death Valley" by Vincent Canby. From *The New York Times Film Reviews* (1969-1970) in *The New York Times,* 13 February 1970. © 1970 by *The New York Times.* Reprinted by permission.

"Did Antonioni Miss the 'Point'?" by Richard Goldstein. From The *New York Times Film Reviews* (1969-1970) in *The New York Times*, 22 February 1970. © 1970 by Richard Goldstein. Reprinted by permission.

Sam Shepard: the Life and Work of an American Dreamer by Ellen Oumano. © 1986 by St. Martin's Press. Reprinted by permission.

"Here Comes the Sun: New Ways of Seeing in Antonioni's *Zabriskie Point*" by Fiona A. Villella. From Senses of Cinema, issue no. 4 [online journal]. Melbourne, Australia [cited March 2000]; available from www.sensesofcinema.com. Reprinted by permission.

"Stage: Sam Shepard Offers 'Buried Child'" by Richard Eder. From *The New York Times Theatre Critics' Reviews* (1978) in *The New York Times*, 7 November 1978. © 1978 by Richard Eder. Reprinted by permission.

"Prodigal Grandson," by Mel Gussow. From The *New York Times Theater Reviews* (1979-80) in *The New York Times*, 25 January 1979. © 1979 by *The New York Times*. Reprinted by permission.

Sam Shepard's Metaphorical Stages by Lynda Hart. © 1987 by Lynda Hart. Reprinted by permission of Greenwood Publishing Group, Inc., Westport, CT.

"Who Was Icarus' Mother? The Powerless Mother Figures in the Plays of Sam Shepard" by Doris Auerbach. © 1988. From *Sam Shepard: A Casebook*, ed. Kimball King. Reproduced by permission of Routledge, Inc., part of Taylor & Francis Group.

Sam Shepard by David J. DeRose. © 1992 by Twayne Publishers. Reprinted by permission of the Gale Group.